THE ART OF PEOPLE

'An invaluable resource full of practical, manageable tips for anyone who deals with people. Which, of course, is all of us' Gretchen Rubin, bestselling author of *Happier at Home* and *Better Than Before*

'Strong people skills are how I built my business. I find it's a common thread among all successful people, and no matter what level your people skills are at today, you will see a dramatic improvement after reading this book!' Barbara Corcoran, star of ABC's *Shark Tank*, entrepreneur and author of *Shark Tales*

'Dave Kerpen has figured out the secrets of being absurdly likeable. Now that he is revealing his methods in a book, he's even more so' A. J. Jacobs, *New York Times* bestselling author of *The Year of Living Biblically, My Life as an Experiment* and *The Know-It-All*

'Smart, funny and immediately usable. In our fast-paced world, we educate and train on technical skills, but neglect the greatest predictor of success: your ability to connect with and influence others. This is one of the few books that might actually get you a promotion – or a successful company of your own' Shawn Achor, happiness researcher and *New York Times* bestselling author of *The Happiness Advantage*

'The world of communication is rapidly shifting. To keep up, you could spend thousands of hours trying to figure out how to win fans and customers using the latest social networks, or you could buy this book, read Kerpen's proven and practical advice, and begin seeing the success you want right away' Chris Guillebeau, *New York Times* bestselling author of *The Happiness of Pursuit* and *The $100 Startup*

'*The Art of People* hands you the tools you need to build meaningful relationships and transform your future' Adam Braun, *New York Times* bestselling author of *The Promise of a Pencil*

'Full of good, sound advice to keep in mind and utilize for better relationships' Lori Greiner, bestselling author, inventor, entrepreneur and TV personality

'*The Art of People* offers terrific tips on becoming a better listener, networker and communicator – the things to be if you want to get ahead and have the success you crave'
Kate White, former editor-in-chief of *Cosmopolitan* and author of *I Shouldn't Be Telling You This*

'If there is one axiom that applies across any and all business, it is that you need to build relationships first, then do business. No one lives this mantra every day more consistently or more effectively than Dave Kerpen. That's why *The Art of People* is such an important and enjoyable read. Dave's insights and unique perspective make this mandatory reading for anyone and everyone interested in how to engage with their customers and build meaningful and valuable relationships. Buy it. Read it!'
Jim McCann, Founder and CEO of 1-800-FLOWERS.COM, Inc.

'Most people who claim to be a "people person" actually aren't. Kerpen's book shows how to actually become one. Thoughtful and inspiring, *The Art of People* is as important for leaders as it is for the rest of us'
Shane Snow, bestselling author of *Smartcuts*

'Forget conferences and seminars and courses. Dave's tips and strategies won't just make you the smartest person in the room; they'll make you the most successful – and most liked – person in the room, too'
Jeff Haden, Contributing Editor, *Inc* Magazine and bestselling author of *Transform*

'This outstanding book is chock-full of powerful strategies that you can use immediately to better yourself and your relationships with others'
Dr Travis Bradberry, #1 bestselling author of *Emotional Intelligence 2.0*

Also by Dave Kerpen

Likeable Social Media
Likeable Business
Likeable Leadership

DAVE KERPEN

THE ART OF PEOPLE

11 Simple People Skills That Will Get You Everything You Want

PORTFOLIO PENGUIN

UK | USA | Canada | Ireland | Australia
India | New Zealand | South Africa

Portfolio Penguin is part of the Penguin Random House group of companies
whose addresses can be found at global.penguinrandomhouse.com

First published in the United States of America by Crown Business 2016
First published in the United Kingdom by Portfolio Penguin 2016
This edition published 2017
007

Printed in Great Britain by Clays Ltd, St Ives plc

A CIP catalogue record for this book is available from the British Library

ISBN: 978-0-241-25078-5

www.greenpenguin.co.uk

Penguin Random House is committed to a sustainable future for our business, our readers and our planet. This book is made from Forest Stewardship Council® certified paper.

This book is dedicated to my ultimate "people": my baby boy,
Seth Franklin Kerpen, and the women around the two Kerpen boys:
my wife, Carrie, and my daughters, Charlotte and Kate.
Thank you all for teaching me so much about people.
I love you all infinity.

Contents

Introduction

People Matter

I had just walked a red carpet behind *American Idol* sensations Clay Aiken and Ruben Studdard at VH1's Big in 2003 Awards, yet I felt as unhappy and unsuccessful as I'd ever felt in my life. I was living in Los Angeles after a four-month appearance on the reality TV show *Paradise Hotel,* and on the surface you'd think I was doing great. I was smack dab in the middle of fifteen minutes of fame, having appeared on thirty-one episodes of a summer network hit, and I was getting paid appearance fees of $5,000 to $10,000 just to show up at malls, night-clubs, and bars. I was attending parties with the likes of Paris Hilton, Jessica Alba, and Kathy Griffin.

I was famous and was making money, but I was miserable. I felt empty and lonely and disconnected. Los Angeles, California, is a difficult town in which to feel genuinely connected to others, and I was struggling with loneliness and depression big-time. A lack of connection to people, in turns out, is very powerful in a bad way.

The moment after walking that red carpet was the wake-up call I needed, and so I made a decision to reconnect. I took my phone out of my pocket and called the one person I wanted to reconnect with more than anyone in the world. I dialed Carrie's number and waited.

Two years earlier, I had met Carrie at the Radio Disney offices in Boston when she took a sales position working opposite my desk. I had been the number one salesperson in the county, until Carrie came along, that is. She dropped me to number two within three months, and we quickly became best friends even though we were rivals at work. In another three months, I had fallen madly in love with her.

There was one slight problem, however: Carrie was married at the time. What do you do when you find your soul mate and she's not available? Well, Carrie moved to New York with her husband to focus on making her marriage work, and I did what anyone with unrequited love would do: I decided to go on a reality TV show to find another soul mate.

Yup, Fox's *Paradise Hotel.* Filmed in a $30 million home in Acapulco, Mexico, the show featured eighteen sexy singles at a luxury resort trying to "hook up or check out." And me.

Staying on the show had been a challenge for me, as I was very different from most of the model/actor cast members and they didn't like me. Yet somehow, week after week, I was able to maneuver my way out of getting voted off during the weekly elimination ceremony, and thirty-one weeks in I was still standing. I had orchestrated my way to the top through careful favor currying and relationship building with both the players (the cast) and the game makers (the producers). I somehow had gotten even people who hated me to vote for me to stay on the show and the real influencers, the producers, to drive a story line that had me there week after week, the lone "nice guy" on the island of pretty boys and girls.

But I was still unhappy. I missed Carrie and felt empty in my work (or lack of work) both during and in the months after the show. When I dialed that number the night after walking the red carpet in Los Angeles, I was hoping to reconnect with the one person I had met who "got" people better than I did.

"Wow, hey, Dave," Carrie replied. "Crazy to hear from you after a year of not talking and watching you on TV. What are you up to?"

"I'm hanging out with the stars of *American Idol,*" I said, secretly trying to maintain a semblance of pride. "And you?"

"I'm hanging out at home. Actually, I'm going through a divorce right now."

"I'm so sorry to hear that, Carrie," I said while doing a fist pump with the hand not holding the phone. "Actually, I have to be in New York to meet with my agent in two weeks," I fibbed.

Two weeks later I was on a flight to New York. One month later I was dating Carrie, and two months later I was moving to New York for her.

Since that phone call I've been fortunate enough to enjoy eleven

amazing years with Carrie by my side, blissful years that have brought me three terrific children, two very successful businesses, and two bestselling books. Although there have been obstacles, challenges, and downtimes, I've been both happier and more successful than in my wildest dreams thanks to Carrie and the many other people I've formed productive, fulfilling relationships with over the last ten years. Not only that, along the way I've learned something invaluable about life, about myself, and about human beings in general: You can't achieve happiness or success in a vacuum; it all hinges on the bonds you build with the people around you.

In my first book, *Likeable Social Media,* I shared a blueprint for being a successful marketer navigating the fast-changing world of social media. In *Likeable Business,* I shared a blueprint for building a successful social business. Now it's time to think bigger. It's time to think about what it takes to be successful in getting everything you want out of your career and your life. I am writing this book to share this blueprint for success with you.

Talent. Luck. Hard work. Courage. Grit. Persistence. I could go on for hours about what others *say* it takes to be successful. But although these things aren't unimportant, what it ultimately comes down to is people. How well do you understand people, how well can you communicate with people, and how well can you get people to do what you want them to do?

People matter. More than anything, in getting what you want in your job, career, and life, the relationships you have with other people, big and small, make all the difference between a dead-end career and an empty existence—like the one that was sucking the life out of me in Los Angeles—and the full life and thriving business I enjoy today.

This is the art of people.

You may think the **hard-driving, take-no-prisoners self-promoter** is the person who ends up on top, but today it is actually the person with the **best people skills** who gets everything she wants at **home**, at **work**, and in **life**.

In my first two books, *Likeable Social Media* and *Likeable Business,* I wrote about how being "likeable" and what that stood for—listening, storytelling, and building relationships based on authenticity and transparency—is critical for success in online marketing (*Likeable Social Media*) and in business (*Likeable Business*). But building relationships and being likeable isn't important just in social media or within a company; it's important out in the wider world, as well. It's important in every single interaction you have with every single one of the people you encounter, from the receptionist at your client's office to your first date, from your boss at work to the influential woman on Twitter who can help you sell more of your product, from the venture capitalist who might invest in your start-up to the guy you went to high school with whom you see only on Facebook now.

This is the art of people.

Whether it's online or offline, the interactions and relationships with the people around you, who these people are, and what they are willing to do for you will determine how successful you will be. Have empty, weak relationships with the people around you and every challenge you face and every obstacle you encounter will feel like trying to push a boulder up a hill on your own. Cultivate authentic, mutually beneficial relationships built on trust, respect, and cooperation and getting the boulder up that hill will feel a lot easier thanks to the team of people pushing behind you. This book will help you with those interactions and relationships because it describes the eleven essential people skills that, when mastered, will help you get more of what you want in any situation.

This is the art of people.

Many of the tools, tricks, and tips contained in this book may surprise you. They certainly often go against typical business and success wisdom. But then, if typical business and success wisdom worked, everyone would be wildly successful, no? The truth is that even if that traditional wisdom once worked, the times have changed. You may think the hard-driving, take-no-prisoners self-promoter is the person who ends up on top, but today it is actually the person with the best people skills who gets everything she wants at home, at work, and in life.

This is the art of people.

Today, people skills are more important than ever; they are the key to getting what you want both at work and outside it. We are constantly connected to one another: Facebook, Twitter, LinkedIn, and other social media have become the primary way we communicate with others. Plus, in today's world there is so much noise, we are trusting personal referrals more than ever; we have a short attention span, and so we are listening to the people who "get us" and whom we trust. As a result, the key to wielding influence and getting what we want is to be the person *others* like, respect, and trust.

This book is going to discuss the eleven people skills I have learned that will change your life at home and at work. Within the description of each major skill, I'll share stories from my life as well as the lives of some of the most successful and influential people in the world to help illustrate my points. We'll begin with a self-assessment available in the appendix, and another available online at ArtofPeopleBook.com. Along the way, we'll learn the eleven key people skills through fifty-three bite-size lessons you can put into practice right now.

A lot of business books are filled with theory, but readers walk away from them wondering what to actually do. This isn't one of those books. Every chapter will close with a set of First Action Steps to Take (FAST). You'll walk away with dozens of practical ideas about how to communicate better with people and get what you want at work and at home.

Before we start, I urge you to take the assessment in Appendix A. It's a take on the Enneagram: a centuries-old personality test to help you understand what values you're most driven by and how others can best communicate with you. This won't change with time, but you should take this quiz so that you'll learn more about how to connect better with others and in turn get others to respect and like you.

One of my core values is responsiveness, and so even though a book is a static, one-way communication channel, if you have comments or questions along the way, I want you to contact me. If you want to scream in anger or applaud with excitement, are baffled by an assertion, or simply want to experience this book by having a conversation with its author, please don't hesitate to contact me. The best way is through Twitter (@DaveKerpen), followed by LinkedIn (DaveLinkedIn.com), but if you want to go old school, you can email me at dave@likeable.com; either way, I promise to get back to you as quickly as I possibly can.

This is the art of people. Let's get started!

1

Understanding Yourself and Understanding People

1. Myers-Briggs Means Nothing; This Means Everything

Ugh, I thought. Another touchy-feely personality activity.

I was on a retreat at the Canyon Ranch resort in Miami with fellow forum members from the Entrepreneurs' Organization, a global network of CEOs that includes some of my best friends in the world. Normally, I'd be having the time of my life at such a retreat, but for me, a Type A personality who's always on the move and never likes to stop, at this time in this particular location I was struggling to stay engaged. *Relax* is not a word I'd ever liked, and after two rounds of yoga and meditation, the last thing I wanted to do was sit through four hours of a personality assessment I had never heard of.

But I braced myself and forced myself to keep an open mind and a positive attitude about the experience. I'm glad I did, because the four hours that followed changed my life and the way I communicate with others and understand myself forever.

"This is the Enneagram," our psychologist instructor, Brad Kerschensteiner, informed the eight of us. "While much less famous than the Myers-Briggs or DISC assessment, it's actually far more reliable than those two or any other personality assessment for that matter, and its wisdom has been used and passed on over centuries."

Now I was intrigued and paying attention. Over the four hours that followed, I picked up a wealth of information about myself and how people can best communicate with me. Moreover, I learned about the nine major motivators for people and how we can best communicate with all people on the basis of their Enneagram types, 1 through 9. As Brad assessed all eight of us and talked to us about our Enneagram types and the communication implications for each one, I was blown away by how accurate it all was. It was like he was reading my mind!

Self-awareness is the **fundamental building block** of the art of people. You can't understand and **influence others** until you fully **understand yourself** at a **deep level**.

In the year that followed, I became increasingly fluent with the Enneagram and its power in helping us understand ourselves as well as others. I administered the Enneagram to my management team, then to my whole staff, and then to my wife's company's whole team as well. I read whole books on the subject. I became totally engrossed with the value of the Enneagram for self-awareness. I also realized the following:

Self-awareness is the fundamental building block of the art of people. You can't understand and influence others until you fully understand yourself at a deep level.

Of course, like any personality assessment, the Enneagram isn't perfect. Any system that classifies people into only nine categories obviously has its limitations. Yet research has shown time and time again that the Myers-Briggs assessment, the most popular personality assessment, is highly flawed and unreliable over time. Take it twice and you'll probably get a different result than you got six months earlier. The results of the Enneagram, in contrast, don't change over time; they give you a sense of what motivates you most, what to look out for as potential detractors, and how people can best communicate with you, and those things are remarkably stable over time.

Before you read any further, turn to Appendix A and take the Enneagram assessment cowritten by Mario Sikora if you haven't already. An internationally recognized speaker and author, Mario is the coauthor of *Awareness to Action: The Enneagram, Emotional Intelligence, and Change* and the author of many articles on personality styles and leadership, performance improvement, and team building. Mario says, "The Enneagram is a great tool to better understand yourself, which in turn can help you take smarter action."

Once you have your score, look at the chart summarizing the nine major Enneagram types, their associated strengths, and the potential pitfalls to look out for. How well these elements resonate with you probably depends on how high your raw numerical score was for your type on the quiz.

For example, I am a strong Enneagram type 3, striving to be outstanding. One of my common pitfalls has been the "I'll Do It" syndrome, or saying yes to every offer, opportunity, and request I get, thinking that the more I accomplish—the more interviews I do, the more projects I agree to, and the more clients I take on—the more outstanding I'll be. This makes me sound like a real go-getter, but it became a real problem earlier in my career as I was stretched too thin and became worn out to the point where even my family life suffered. That is, it was a problem until I changed the script in my head according to my Enneagram assessment. If I said yes to fewer things, I realized, I could be more outstanding in the things I said yes to. It wasn't easy (fellow Threes out there can sympathize with me, I'm sure), but now I am able to say no to opportunities to speak or do interviews so that I can be more outstanding at other things. I rewrote the script once I understood what really motivates me, and you can do the same thing.

What are your pitfalls based on your Enneagram type? Choose the one that resonates most with you and keep it in mind as you read this book. By the end, I guarantee you'll have a better understanding of how to rewrite the script in light of all you've learned about how you communicate with others and how others communicate with you.

Now that you have a better understanding of yourself from the Enneagram, including your strengths and weaknesses in communication, it's time to take one more quiz: the PeopleStrengths quiz. We developed this assessment to help you understand, among the eleven essential people skills you'll learn in these pages, where your top strengths lie and where you may need more help. Take this now online at ArtofPeopleQuiz.com.

So are you a People-Pleaser? A People-Leader? A People-Guru? Or a People-Persuader? Whichever category you're in, we all know we have lots of room for improvement when it comes to dealing with and influencing people. The great news is that you've already begun the improvement process by getting to know yourself a little better than you did before you picked up this book.

Of course, there are hundreds of other assessments you can take to understand yourself and your strengths and weaknesses. I happen to be a huge fan of the Enneagram because it's time-tested, simple, and reliable, and of the People Strengths Quiz because, well, I wrote it. But of course, whatever your particular assessment is, the important takeaway is this:

The first step in learning how to better influence others to get what you want in your career and in life is to understand yourself.

The better you understand yourself—your unconscious motivations, what gets you up and what gets you down, what makes you tick, and how you best interact with others—the better off you'll be at understanding other people and getting them to do things for you.

FAST **F**irst **A**ction **S**teps to **T**ake:

1. Complete the Enneagram quiz in Appendix A if you haven't already done that.
2. Write down three people-related weaknesses you want to work on. Write down a solution for each one in light of your core Enneagram assessment.
3. Write down your greatest strength. How can you improve on it as you read this book?

2. How to "Get" Anyone (Even If You Don't Like Him)

"I just don't get him," I muttered to myself after hanging up the phone. I had just finished a phone call with the senior person at a company that was an important business partner of ours, and I felt frustrated, angry, and confused. We had been struggling to get this business partnership off the ground for months, and I believed I had key insights into understanding why and helping rectify the problem. But John (as we'll call him) just didn't want to listen to me or cooperate or be helpful in any way.

John was mean and grumpy, and I just didn't get him. He seemed to have a huge chip on his shoulder, was angry at the world, and was determined to plow down anyone who stood in his way. He seemed a lot like the hard-driving, take-no-prisoners self-promoter I described in Chapter 1, good at making orders but not good at making relationships. In several face-to-face meetings I had never once seen him even hint at a smile.

The first step in influencing people is understanding them, and I simply didn't understand John. I had tried for months to connect with him, but to no avail. How could I work effectively with someone I didn't like? How could I work with someone I didn't even understand?

Feeling utterly defeated, I approached my wife, Carrie, with the problem: "I just don't get this man, Carrie. What can I do?"

Carrie, the person who gets people better than anyone I've ever met, replied right away: "If you say you don't get him, you'll definitely never get him."

We all have people we don't get at first or maybe ever. Everyone's different, and sometimes it's hard to understand people who are very different from ourselves. Many times that may be okay because you may not need to interact with some person you don't get, but often it does matter. If you're ever going to want or need to have a meaningful or productive interaction with someone, whether it's a colleague at work, a client of your business, or a cousin at family gatherings, it pays to figure out a way to get that person.

Step 1, as Carrie shared with me, is to refuse to believe that you can't. No matter how different a person is, no matter how you may feel when you're around her, no matter what her actions are, you have to believe that with some effort you will be able to understand her.

Self-determination is a powerful force, and once you refuse to say "I don't get him," you'll be better off. But that alone isn't enough.

"Take him out for coffee," Carrie suggested about John, the man I was now determined to get.

"But I absolutely loathe him," I replied, cringing at the thought.

"See it as an experiment, then," Carrie said. "An experiment to see if you can understand someone very different from you. Ask questions, then shut up and listen."

As much as I protested, Carrie's advice, as usual, turned out to be spot-on. Two weeks and one coffee later, I got John. I still didn't like him very much, but after sitting down with him for coffee outside the office and getting the opportunity to talk (and listen) face-to-face for just thirty minutes, I really did feel that I understood where John was coming from. As it turns out, John had had a tough stretch of several years as a child with just one parent, and it seemed that somewhere along the way he had decided to become fiercely independent. John was unmistakably an Enneagram type 8—driven to be powerful—and sometimes that drive for independence could make him abrasive and standoffish and generally tough to be around.

John's behaviors didn't change as a result of our meeting, of course, but just a little bit of understanding made a big difference in my future interactions with him. Over the weeks that followed, our conversations got more congenial, and we actually made some progress toward driving the mutual business results we were both looking for. He even cracked a smile at one face-to-face meeting a few months later. I ended up getting most of what I wanted out of the business dealings and the relationship.

I never would have had that opportunity, though, if I had resigned myself to the fact that I didn't get John and left it at that. Who do *you* work with whom you just don't get? Who do you come into contact with on a regular basis whom you can't seem to understand no matter how much you scratch your head?

The first step is to insist that you can *get that person. The next step is to invest fifteen minutes and five dollars in having a cup of coffee with that person.*

You may not walk away understanding the person completely or even liking him any better. But you'll have a fighting chance to build a more productive and beneficial relationship from then on.

John, wherever you are today, I hope you're still enjoying your coffee black and occasionally cracking a smile.

FAST First **A**ction **S**teps to **T**ake:

1. Write down the names of three people in your life whom you're struggling to get.
2. Commit to asking one to have coffee with you after you finish this chapter.
3. Walk into the coffee meeting determined to get this person (even if you still don't like her).

3. How to Understand Someone Better Than You Do Your Friends (in Just Three Minutes)

"Now you're going to get to know the person next to you better than you know many of your friends, in just three minutes with just three questions!" said the tall, enthusiastic speaker on stage in front of 1,200 people.

I sat in the front row, excited but dubious about the claim that Larry Benet had just made at the Social Media Marketing World conference in spring 2013. Larry is a man on a networking mission. Often referred to as one of the "Most Connected People on the Planet," Larry Benet builds much more than just passing friendships. He has earned a sterling reputation as a master relationship builder as well as a thought-provoking and highly entertaining seminar speaker.

But this was my first experience with Larry Benet, and I must admit that I was a doubter. Larry was the first keynote speaker at the conference, and I knew he was there to teach people how to network better. Still, the notion that he could teach me to understand someone better than I know many of my friends in three minutes seemed a bit far-fetched even for an expert.

"Question number one: What is the most exciting thing you're working on right now? On your marks, get set, go!" Larry said confidently.

I turned to my left and very quickly introduced myself to the man next to me. We didn't have much time, so I quickly told Steven about Likeable Local, the new company I was getting ready to launch, and he told me about a science project in a box his company was about to unveil. Whew, just under the deadline.

"Question number two!" Larry's big voice bellowed from the center of the stage. "If you had enough money to retire and then some, what would you be doing?"

The pressure was on with only a minute to share answers, and so I quickly learned that Steven would travel the world with his wife, going to all seven continents, and I said that I would run for office, perhaps for mayor of New York City or governor of the state. Again, we made it in just under a minute. This was proving to be a very interesting experiment!

"Final question, and remember, you have just a minute to both answer it," Larry announced. "What is your favorite charity organization to support and why?"

I insisted that Steven go first this time, because I had two organizations I wished to talk about and wanted to make sure he got his in. He told me about the Nature Conservancy (Nature.org) and how passionately he felt about conversation and climate change, and I told him about the Multiple Sclerosis Society and the National Alliance for Mental Illness and how with multiple family members affected, my wife and I felt compelled to support both organizations.

And that was it. Steven and I didn't immediately become best friends after this exchange. We didn't continue the conversation over dinner or invite each other over to meet our respective families. Although Steven and I exchanged a few emails after the event, it's been over two years since that first and only conversation I had with him. But here's the really interesting thing: It's been over two years, yet I still recall with ease the contents of that conversation. I still know more about Steven after three minutes over two years ago than I do about most of my casual friends from high school, college, and work.

After informally surveying the audience and smugly determining that the doubters like me had been persuaded, Larry continued with his keynote. He told the audience that life's too short to waste precious minutes on small talk about the weather or where people are from or what they do for a living. He argued that if we could get to know the person sitting next to us as well as we had in just three minutes, why shouldn't we give ourselves and the people we meet the same gift in future encounters?

Larry Benet was absolutely right. When we meet people "in real life" we may open up a conversation with a bit of small talk because it's far more socially acceptable than asking pointed questions. But the truth is that by asking better, smarter questions, we can understand the people we meet much more quickly and determine rapidly whether they're friend or foe, a potential business partner or mate, a future employee or casual acquaintance. Life is short. The less time we waste on the weather, the better.

The three questions Larry taught me are excellent ones. That said, there are lots of other questions you can ask early in a first encounter with someone to better understand that person and his or her worldview. Here are ten questions for your consideration:

1. What is the most exciting thing in your professional life right now?
2. What is the most exciting thing in your personal life right now?
3. If you had enough money to retire, what would you be doing today?
4. What's one thing you would like to be doing or would like to have five years from now?
5. What's your favorite charity organization to support and why?
6. If you weren't doing what you do today, what would you be doing and why?
7. Other than a member of your family, tell me about your role model.
8. Who's been the most important influence on you?
9. How would your favorite teacher describe you?
10. If you could choose to do anything for a day, what would it be and why?

These questions not only break the ice, they quickly get people talking about the things that really matter, the things that will reveal their true personalities: their values, their likes, their hopes, and their passions. Although you can't administer a personality test to someone you've just met, you can ask better questions than the standard "Where are you from?" "Where did you go to school?" "What do you do?" and "How do you like this weather?"

At this point perhaps some of you are thinking, "Dave, you were told by a conference speaker to ask these questions. I can't just come out to someone I've just met and ask these sorts of things without people giving me a crazy look."

You may be right, and so when it comes time to put this experiment into action for yourself, you can simply open with, "I just read this crazy book that talked about asking better questions when you first meet someone. Mind if we try out a couple of these questions and each answer them?"

You'll be surprised how easily the conversation goes and how valuable it is, just as I was surprised the day I met Larry Benet. And you'll start understanding people a lot better and faster, too.

FAST **F**irst **A**ction **S**teps to **T**ake:

1. Write down your favorite four questions from the list of ten above.
2. The next time you meet someone at work or in a social setting, try out two or three of them.
3. Note how much better you can break the ice and get to know someone by using better questions.

4. Be Interested Instead of Interesting

When I recently picked up my friend Danny at the airport, we'd barely pulled out of the parking space before he enthusiastically told me, "I just met the nicest woman on the planet on my plane!" Danny wasn't normally a very excitable guy, and so I knew he had met someone really great.

"Awesome," I responded. "What was her name?"

"You know, I'm not sure," he told me, a bit embarrassed in light of his previous statement.

"Okay, then," I continued. "What does she do for a living?"

"I don't recall," he replied.

I continued to ask questions about this mystery "nicest woman on the planet" until my friend admitted, "Actually, I guess I did most of the talking. Okay, maybe I did just about all of the talking."

We humans love to talk. Just about all of us would rather talk about ourselves than listen in any one-on-one social situation. There's nothing wrong with that; it just is what it is. People inherently care a lot more about themselves and their families than they care about you, and certainly if you are a relative stranger, they care way more about themselves than they care about you or anything you have to say.

Again, there's nothing inherently wrong with or even surprising about that fact, but it is a fact. The sooner you can embrace that reality—just about no stranger cares about you or what you have to say nearly as much as she cares about herself and what she has to say—the sooner you will get better at establishing relationships with people and wielding influence with them.

Since humans love to talk about themselves, if you can focus on listening, truly listening, attentively to the person you're with, that person will appreciate you, like you, or even adore you the way Danny adored the stranger on the plane. Even if you don't say a thing, as long as you continue to acknowledge that you're listening, using eye contact and body language and the occasional "Uh huh" and "I know," that person will adore you. This may be the easiest technique in this whole book! The secret to getting people to adore you is to shut up and listen.

As simple as this may sound, it's true; although there is one major caveat: You can't *passively* listen as if this were a parlor trick you learned from a book. By that I mean that you can't do what many of us do when we think we're listening, which is sit there waiting to talk. You have to *actively* listen and authentically care about the person who is talking to you. You have to genuinely focus. But if you can do this (and it takes practice), it will help you curry favor with and strengthen relationships with people every single time.

Just resist the temptation to talk about yourself. Even if you are asked questions, deflect or answer them quickly and then give the other person an immediate opportunity to talk again. Since most of us do love to talk, this may go against your natural inclination. If you find active listening challenging, the best way to practice is by practicing silence, as difficult as that may be. I love public speaking, private speaking, and, like all humans, talking about myself, and so I get how hard this is. But every time I do it, it gets easier.

Airplanes provide the perfect opportunity to practice this skill. Turn to the person next to you on a flight and start asking questions. Listen, listen, and then listen some more. Follow up authentically with statements such as "Tell me more about that." You'll be shocked at how quickly and how deeply you can get to know that person just by letting him talk about himself.

The **secret** to getting people to **adore you** is to **shut up** and **listen**.

But this technique isn't just about making a new friend. It's about increasing the chances that you'll get something out of relationships. Whether it's today, tomorrow, or five years from now, you'll be much better positioned to ask a favor of, get a tip from, or do business with this individual—all because you sat back and listened. For example, two years ago on a cross-country flight, I sat next to an attorney named Steven. I asked him a lot of questions and got him talking about his life, his goals, his kids, and his dreams. We didn't have a ton in common, but I appreciated genuinely getting to know someone. At the end of the flight, we exchanged contact information. A year and a half later, he became a small investor in one of my companies.

Shutting up and listening works in understanding strangers, but it works even better in understanding friends and colleagues. Case in point: Three years ago, I tried this tactic at my company when I announced before a Likeable senior management meeting that I wouldn't be speaking at that meeting no matter what. At first some (including me) were shocked that I intended only to sit back and listen, but when I did, I gained more insight into our business and its senior executives in just one hour than I had in weeks. And they felt more understood, empowered, and respected than ever before—and it made them like me better as a boss, as well!

The efficacy of this tactic was demonstrated once more last year when I went on a leadership retreat with several close entrepreneur friends. Our leader suggested we have a "silent breakfast," and I liked it so much, I decided to remain silent for several hours afterward. Not only was I way more attuned to the people and environment around me, I was also more appreciated. One close friend said to me, perhaps jokingly, "You know, Dave, I really like you a lot more when you're silent than when you're talking."

Remember that people care more about themselves than they care about you. People want to talk about themselves. Listening and letting people talk is key to winning them over in life, in business, and in all human relationships. Once you can tap into people's desire to talk about themselves and feel listened to, you'll be able to build more rapport with and eventually influence everyone you know and meet.

The famed author and speaker Dale Carnegie said, "You can make more friends in two months by becoming interested in other people than you can in two years by trying to get other people interested in you."

Allow me to paraphrase: In the field of influence, it is more important to be interested than to be interesting.

If you don't believe me, I urge you to practice. Just give it a try, even for one conversation, and tweet me (@DaveKerpen) with your experience. I'll be listening.

FAST First **A**ction **S**teps to **T**ake:

1. On a plane or train ride, practice turning to a stranger and asking questions and actually listening to the answers without jumping in and saying something about yourself.
2. Spend at least one conversation at work or at home focusing 90 percent or more on asking genuine questions and listening versus talking. Prepare your audience ahead of time if that makes you feel more comfortable. Afterward, note your experience and ask your conversation partner or partners about their experience.

5. Most People Are Lonely; Help Them Feel Connected

Robin Williams was one of the most celebrated actors and most successful personalities of all time. Millions of people admired him, thousands knew and loved him, and dozens felt close to him. Yet in August 2014 Robin Williams took his own life. Despite all that love and success, Williams was profoundly lonely.

The same night Robin Williams died, I attended a party at a bar in downtown New York City to support an editor friend of mine. With my wife having gone home already, I planned to make a quick appearance at the party, say hi to my friend, and leave. But I needed to charge my cell phone before heading home, and so I asked someone at the party where I could charge it. She sent me downstairs, where I plugged in the phone and sat down on a couch to wait. Next to me sat Jackie, a thirty-one-year-old employee of one of the sponsors of the party, who had consumed a few alcoholic beverages before I sat down.

"Tell me about yourself," I said to Jackie, and that really was all I had to say. In the twenty minutes that followed, while my phone's battery charged, I learned Jackie's story. Always the bridesmaid, never the bride, Jackie was sad not to have a partner with whom to share her life. She had achieved great success in her career, rising through the ranks at her current company, but she told me that something was missing. Jackie told me about her career ambitions and her fears and challenges. She told me about her dreams and her goals and her love of travel—and nearly every place she'd ever traveled to.

I had barely said a thing except my initial "Tell me about yourself" and then a few words to acknowledge that I was listening. Yet Jackie opened up to me as if we were the best of friends. Perhaps she was lonely, perhaps she was really seeking a connection; it's hard to say for sure. But what happened next was truly shocking.

"You were really great to talk to," I said. "But I'm afraid I've got to get going." I turned to the outlet to retrieve my phone, and Jackie realized she'd been doing all the talking.

"Oh, my goodness, I'm so sorry. I haven't asked a thing about you. Traveling anywhere interesting soon?" asked a sobering-up Jackie.

"Actually, I'm going to San Francisco next week for my wife's birthday."

"Oh, I love San Francisco!" she replied. "I'm there all the time for work."

"Got any connections to French Laundry by chance?" I asked. You see, I had been trying to get into the exclusive Napa Valley fine dining establishment for months in the lead-up to the trip.

"As a matter of fact, I do!" Jackie replied enthusiastically. "Let me make a phone call and see what I can do."

The next week I was dining in style with my wife in Yountville, tasting scrumptious delights at one of the hardest-to-get-into restaurants in the country. On one hand, I had done nothing but ask a stranger for help to get this special unexpected night. On the other hand, I had dedicated real time—twenty minutes of my life—to helping fill a void of loneliness in someone's life, something that perhaps rarely happened for her.

Listen to understand, authentically try to connect deeply with people, help them feel less lonely, and you will find yourself far more able to influence them.

The key to this lesson, as in many of the lessons in this book, is to do this *authentically*. This means not helping people feel less lonely in order to influence them but because it's the right thing to do. I had no idea, of course, that Jackie had connections at French Laundry. I didn't even expect the topic to come up in conversation. Instead, I listened and connected and helped her feel less lonely, if only for a few moments, and that happened to lead to my getting exactly what I most wanted at the time.

Even the most well-adjusted, psychologically healthy individuals have moments when they feel lonely and long to be more connected to other human beings. By approaching people with the intent to understand them and more deeply connect to them, we differentiate ourselves from most people in the world, who don't care or are too busy worrying about their own problems to spend time focusing on others. When we *do* focus on others and help them feel less lonely, a world of opportunities opens up for us.

FAST First **A**ction **S**teps to **T**ake:

1. Practice this with three people: two relative strangers and one friend or family member. With each person, ask questions, listen, and seek to understand and connect with that person on a deeper level.
2. Initiate at least one conversation at work in which you ask about deeper topics than you'd normally discuss (if appropriate). Let the other person be a bit vulnerable and share your own vulnerability as well. Note afterward whether you feel a stronger connection with this person and whether you'd feel more comfortable asking him for something another day.

2

Meeting the Right People

6. Wear Orange Shoes: The Simple Keys to Networking That Nobody Talks About

Frustrated, annoyed, and nearly ready to give up.

That was how I felt as I wandered around during the happy hour at the end of the Founders start-up event. I had attended in part to learn, and I had indeed learned a lot at the sessions all day. But my primary reason had been to meet people, including potential investors in my start-up.

In that objective I had come up short. There were dozens of investors in the room, but their time had been hoarded by other start-ups, and the one I managed to meet had brushed me off without really considering my pitch. But that was okay, because there was really only one person I'd come to see: Dave McClure.

Dave McClure was the founding partner of 500 Startups, a well-respected start-up fund based in Silicon Valley with offices all over the world. I recently had received an all-important email introduction to Dave through Victoria Ransom, the cofounder of the Wildfire app (sold to Google) and a mutual friend, but thus far my email had gone unanswered. I knew Dave was at the event, because he had been one of the speakers that afternoon. This was my chance to connect with him in the flesh.

I stood in a room filled with entrepreneurs and investors, hoping to get the attention of just one. I was contemplating whether to get a drink from the bar, when all of a sudden I heard, "I have got to talk to the man wearing those fucking shoes!"

I looked up, and there was Dave McClure. Of the three hundred people in the room, the one I wanted to talk to the most was actually stopping *me* to chat. Why? He had noticed my bright orange sneakers, and in a room filled with people dying to talk to him, my sneakers were the reason he had decided to initiate a conversation with me. This was my chance, and I wasn't going to waste it.

"Hope they're bright enough for you, Dave," I replied jokingly, and proceeded to take the opportunity to remind him about the recent email introduction and tell him a bit more about our business. Within fifteen minutes he had introduced me to his New York partner, Shai Goldman, and we had set up a time for a follow-up meeting. A few weeks later, 500 Startups became a key investor in our tech start-up, Likeable Local.

Were my orange shoes the reason I secured an investment? Of course not. But they *were* the reason I got into a conversation in the first place. In a room full of people trying to get busy people's attention, that was all it took to stand out in the crowd.

The orange shoes I wore that day were the twenty-first pair I've owned, and I'm now up to twenty-nine pairs of orange sneakers and shoes. Not a day goes by that I don't wear orange shoes. And it's not just conferences where they make me stand out and create more opportunities to meet people. It's in ordinary moments: on the train to and from work, at coffee shops, and in building lobbies. People walk up to me nearly every day, comment on the shoes, and begin a conversation. Some of those conversations lead to nothing, but others lead to exciting opportunities, real relationships, and connections with people who can add value to my life in some way. Without those shoes, I might have never met those people.

Of course, this doesn't mean you should go out and purchase twenty-nine pairs of orange shoes (or any color shoes, for that matter; shoes are expensive). But you have an opportunity to create a signature style that will help you stand out at conferences and elsewhere and give you an opportunity to meet more people.

Orange shoes are my thing, but yours can be anything; the only two criteria are that it be attention-grabbing and that it feel authentic to you. If it's not shoes, is it a scarf? Earrings? A noticeable briefcase or tie? A watch, a hat, or a bracelet, perhaps? What can your signature style be at conferences and beyond? How can you become more noticeable and not only stand out in a crowd but actually attract people to you?

Some people may dismiss this idea as silly. Some may not want to stand out like a sore thumb in a crowd. To them I say the following: You don't need to look foolish to have a signature style. Even if your signature style doesn't include bright, noticeable colors, if you're consistent in your style, you'll be much more likely to be remembered by the people you meet. Think about it this way: Why *not* gain any edge you can over everyone else in the room?

FAST **F**irst **A**ction **S**teps to **T**ake:

1. Write down a list of three to five possible accessories, colors, and/or items you can adopt as your signature stand-out style.
2. Ask three people you know and trust about your list. Which do they think is the most winning style?
3. Purchase the item or items necessary to create your signature style and begin rocking the new look at the next event you attend.

7. How to Meet Just About Anyone

"You can't possibly get a meeting with her," my colleague said of Sallie Krawcheck, the tough-as-nails former CEO of Merrill Lynch, known as the most powerful woman on Wall Street. I had always admired Sallie's transparency and persistence and her reputation as an incredibly smart leader.

"Why not?" I asked, sensing a challenge and therefore an opportunity. I recently had read a thought-provoking article by Sallie and had decided I wanted to meet her. I wasn't sure how or why exactly, but hearing from a colleague that I couldn't do something was the best way to ensure that I'd do it or at least go down trying.

I turned to the online social network that already had connected me to dozens of leaders throughout the world. No, I didn't turn to Facebook, the world's largest social network. Nor did I turn to Twitter, the world's most open social network. Instead, I turned to the network built exclusively for the world's professionals: LinkedIn.

A quick search for mutual connections uncovered three dozen, and I chose one, a friend named Sergio who worked as a high-ranking executive at General Electric at that time, to seek an introduction. I had done a free workshop for Sergio years before, and I knew he'd remember me fondly from that day and be eager to return the favor. When looking for an introduction through mutual connections on LinkedIn, I always look for people whom I've done favors for and who are likely to have influence with the person I want to meet. I quickly typed out an introduction request to Sergio and went on with my day.

A few hours later, I got an email saying I was connected to Sallie on LinkedIn, and so I reached out to Sallie, saying I was a big fan and suggesting we could both benefit from a meeting. A week later we were sitting across from each other over cups of coffee.

Sallie and I talked about business, about leadership, and about LinkedIn, among other things. Since that first meeting, I've seen Sallie several more times; spoken in front of employees at a new company she owns, Ellevate Network; and introduced her to my wife, whose podcast she's appeared on. I'm still not sure what will come of our professional relationship, but that's not the point.

The point is that I admired her, wanted to meet her, and, thanks to the right request to the right person and a few clicks on LinkedIn, did just that. I've also connected in this way to Brad Smith, the CEO of the Fortune 500 payroll company Intuit; Doug Conant, the chairman of Avon; Claire Diaz-Ortiz, the early Twitter employee who got the Pope and Hillary Clinton on Twitter; and thousands more business leaders, authors, and highly motivated professionals. I'm never sure exactly how I can benefit people when I connect to them or how they can benefit me, but I'm confident that by connecting to lots of smart, interesting, well-connected people, I'll best position myself to meet the people I need to meet in the future to get what I want. With over 15,000 connections, 500,000 followers, and 10 million second-degree connections on LinkedIn, I know there are very few people I can't connect with and meet with just a few clicks.

Here's the blueprint for success on the world's more important social network:

1. Create a full profile, with attention given to every school you've been to, organization you've worked at, and professional group you've been in. The more you put in your profile, the more you'll potentially have in common with the people you want to connect with, and there are few better ways to open an introductory email than by mentioning some experience or affiliation that you share.
2. Connect with all of the people you went to school with and have worked with. This will give you more connections,

but more important, it will optimize the number of second-degree connections you have on the network.

3. Any time you want to meet someone, look that person up on LinkedIn, find a mutual connection, and write to the mutual connection asking for an introduction. If you don't share a first-degree connection, you probably share a second-degree connection; that makes this process a bit more difficult but still quite possible.
4. Once you get connected, set up a meeting with your new connection.

If this process sounds simple, that's because it really is. Although it doesn't *always* work (Bill Gates has yet to get back to me, for instance), it's a powerful way to meet just about anyone in the world you want to meet. I can honestly say that the people I've connected with and met through LinkedIn collectively have changed my life. Whom could you meet who would change yours?

FAST First **A**ction **S**teps to **T**ake:

1. Write down a list of three to five professionals who could change your life whom you'd love to connect with.
2. Follow the steps listed above to optimize your LinkedIn profile. Include photos, links, videos, and SlideShare presentations wherever possible.
3. Solicit intros to your dream pros of choice. Remember to take into account the influence your mutual connection is likely to have and the amount of social capital (have you done favors for this person in the past?) you've earned before asking for an introduction.

8. Create Your Own Advisory Board

"It's not fair," I complained. "Why can't I have a mentor? Just because I'm the boss, that doesn't mean there aren't lots of people I can learn from in our industry."

I was chatting with my friend Andy, a fellow entrepreneur, and lamenting the fact that I had just set up a formal mentoring program at our company. However, because I was the person at the top, there was nobody to mentor me.

"Don't be silly," replied Andy. "You're an entrepreneur, for God's sake. Think of a creative solution to the problem. Why not set up an advisory board?"

My first reaction was shock. Advisory boards were for large, established companies with lots of resources. How could I create an advisory board for my little venture? But I was sufficiently intrigued. "Why shouldn't I have the same opportunities big-company CEOs have?" I wondered. "I should! Let me take matters into my own hands."

The hard part was figuring out how.

I researched advisory boards: their structures, their purposes, their typical size and shape, and how to form them. Over the course of my research, I learned that a key distinction between boards of directors and advisory boards is that whereas boards of directors are formal legal entities that in fact govern organizations, advisory boards can be totally informal and can be anything we want them to be for any purpose we choose.

The first step, I decided, was to figure out what the purpose of my advisory board would be. I decided it would be to help run my wife's and my social media agency and potentially help us launch a software company. I then began thinking about all the people I knew who potentially could help in either way, tracked them down, and made the asks. Since I was asking very busy people to make a commitment to me, I vowed to provide all my advisers with something of value in return. First, I'd pay them: their choice annually of a small cash stipend or a small piece of equity in our company. But that alone felt too impersonal, so I didn't stop there. Since I was asking each adviser to attend four quarterly board meetings, I promised to offer a leadership training exercise and buy dinner at each one. I also told them I hoped I could offer them networking opportunities to one another as well. In exchange, at each meeting, I'd share one or two challenges I was going through and ask for everyone's relevant experience and advice in tackling similar situations.

I was hoping for an advisory board of five to seven people, and so I ended up asking eleven people to serve, assuming that about half would turn me down. I used my large network to find people across different disciplines and backgrounds, people I had met socially through the years, people I had worked for and with, and people I didn't know at all except through other people.

Much to my astonishment, all the people I asked said yes, and so I ended up with a much larger advisory board than I'd planned. Aside from the challenge of scheduling eleven people four times a year, it's been an amazing experience. Currently, my advisory board is made up of people such as Ed Zuckerberg, Mark's dad and a super-successful business owner in his own right; Nihal Mehta, four-time serial entrepreneur turned venture capitalist; and Chris McCann, president of 1-800-Flowers.com, among other terrific finance, legal, and brand-marketing minds. Each quarter, we've gotten together in a conference room at our office and sat for two or three hours talking. Usually we begin with a twenty-minute icebreaker, team-building exercise, or leadership training activity, followed by a business and financial update and a question-and-answer period. Then I share one or two of my challenges, after which we go around the room and everyone weighs in with his or her thoughts, experiences, and counsel. The members of my advisory board have been game changers in helping me tackle problems I've really needed help with and achieve things I've really wanted, including launching that software company. Three years ago, I found my own mentoring program, and I haven't looked back since.

This might make a lot of sense to you if you're an entrepreneur or small-business owner. But what if you're not? Remember my research, which found that anyone can set up an advisory board for any purpose. A year ago, I was talking to my friend Dorie Clark, bestselling author and personal branding consultant, and she agreed completely: "I recommend that everyone form their own personal advisory board," she told me.

Whether you're a stay-at-home mom trying to figure out what to do next with your life, a young gun quickly climbing the corporate ladder, or a fifty-five-year-old teacher thinking about a career change, you, too, deserve an advisory board. No matter who you are and what you do for a living, a well-constructed advisory board can help you take the next steps to grow personally and professionally. The board can help challenge you, guide you, and teach you. Although I recommend working as I did to provide value to each adviser at each meeting, I learned that it's been my success that has made my advisers feel most rewarded.

The most important things to keep in mind in creating and maintaining a successful advisory board are to choose your advisers carefully and to build and keep a solid structure for the meetings. The more seriously you take this endeavor, the more seriously your advisers will. If you call up a couple of friends spontaneously and ask them to meet you at the local diner for coffee to talk over an issue you're having, that's not an advisory board. But if you carefully select people you admire and respect—people whom you've met over the years or whom you might have access to through someone you already know (see Chapter 7)—and gather them three to six times a year for scheduled meetings in a quiet room with an agenda that you stick to, well, that's an advisory board.

I've found that the best thing about having an advisory board is the multiplier effect. It's great to have even one smart person thinking about how to help you, but when you have multiple smart people in the same room at the same time trying to help you, the results are powerful. People think of new ideas and form connections that they wouldn't have thought of otherwise, and everyone ends up benefiting. If you're doing this well, you'll be providing so much value for your advisory board that you might not even need to compensate them financially (this is important if they're a personal advisory board and not a business one).

Remember, you can form an advisory board for any purpose, duration, or idea that you choose. The key is to find and recruit smart, experienced people in whatever area you'd like to focus on. Looking to start a business? Build an advisory board of successful entrepreneurs. Looking to make senior partner at a law firm? Build an advisory board of senior attorneys and relevant clients. Looking to figure out what you want to do in the next chapter of your life? Build an advisory board of people with lots of varied experience who really know you.

Everybody deserves mentors, and everyone can have them. It's up to you to take matters into your own hands and make an advisory board happen.

FAST First **A**ction **S**teps to **T**ake:

1. Write down two or three goals for what an advisory board could help you with over time.
2. Brainstorm a list of seven to eleven people who could serve on your advisory board and help you with those goals. At least half

of them should be people you've met, and at least two should be people you've never met but could perhaps meet through connections.

3. Determine your preferred meeting format, structure, frequency, and location as well as the compensation you plan to offer, if any.

4. Start contacting people and invite them to be on your advisory board.

9. Hire Slow and Fire Fast—at Work *and* in Life

Dave," my general manager, Sam, said over the phone to me, "you're going to want to sit down for this one."

"Okay," I replied, sitting down in my home office. I had been working there that day because one of my daughters was home sick from school, and I wasn't looking forward to what I was about to hear.

"We found cocaine in the men's room. We think it's Payton's. We have a witness. I'm really sorry to be the messenger."

Upon hearing this I quickly went through a series of emotions: shock (How could this happen at my office?), followed by denial (This can't be happening), followed by anger (How dare he do this at our office?), followed by sadness (I can't believe I've let this toxic culture develop). I had waited too long, but I wasn't going to wait a moment longer.

Payton (the name has been changed to protect the guilty) was a sales manager. Like many new hires, he started off very promisingly, full of energy, passion, and commitment. But I had quickly realized that something wasn't right. He was too salesy, too over the top, just *too much.* Rumors developed that he had a drug problem. More rumors developed that he was getting drunk with people who reported to him, and there were reports about inappropriate remarks he had made to members of the opposite sex. Some of the early customers Payton and his team sold to had canceled recently, saying they were overpromised.

I knew we had a major problem pretty early. But I'm embarrassed to admit that I didn't act on that knowledge nearly as quickly as I should have. I wanted to give Payton the benefit of the doubt; I wanted it to work out, wanted to believe I had made a good hire. Therefore, under the pretense of coaching him to success, I kept Payton on.

But once I heard about the cocaine in the men's room, I realized things had gone too far. I called a neighbor to come look after my sneezing child and hopped onto the next train into the city to go to our office. After a quick meeting with Payton and someone from human resources, he was gone from our company, and from my life, forever.

This is probably the most dramatic case of my not firing someone fast enough, but far from the only one. There have been many times I've brought on someone I was excited about, only to quickly learn, once he was on the job, that he was not right. Sometimes the employee can simply move seats to another role and thrive there. But usually if it feels like it's not a fit, there's a reason for that and it's best for both parties if they agree to part ways.

"Hire slow, fire fast" is a popular adage in business circles because great leaders realize that the wrong employee in the wrong seat can be truly toxic to an organization. That's why you've got to work hard to find the right people and absolutely take your time to hire, but as soon as you know in your gut that it's not going to work out, it's time to cut bait.

This isn't true only in business, however. It's equally true outside of business, in all relationships.

Think about it: How many times have you kept at it in a relationship, kept giving the other person a chance, hoping he or she would change, only to give up on the relationship eventually and move on, all the while kicking yourself for waiting so long?

We humans hate admitting when we've made a mistake. In my situation with Payton, I wanted to believe I had made a good hire. Therefore, despite strong consistent signals to the contrary, I kept him on, kept working on the relationship, kept hoping for change rather than face the brutal facts. This is a mind trick that we have to be aware of, called *cognitive dissonance.* We want to believe we've made good decisions, and so even after receiving data that tell us we haven't, we tend to refuse to recognize the data or it takes us a long time to do so. That's obviously a problem, and potentially a toxic one in key relationships in our lives.

It's especially important to hire slow and fire fast in our lives outside work. What does this mean? Be cautious when getting into relationships—whether romantic, platonic, or otherwise—with people. Don't completely give away your trust and heart to someone you've just met. It's okay—heck, as someone who's been in love a few times and is still madly in love with my wife can vouch, even great—eventually to jump full-throttle into a new relationship, to let yourself be completely vulnerable, transparent, and trusting. But that doesn't mean you should bury your head in the sand. If you start to feel in your gut that the relationship is not right, there's a reason. Look at the cold hard facts and data and watch out for that little voice that whispers, "Stick with it; you made the right decision." That's your cognitive dissonance talking.

I've seen people stick around for years in unhealthy relationships with partners or with toxic employees or business partners despite knowing better. Change is hard, and cognitive dissonance is a powerful phenomenon. But the truth is that every minute spent with a toxic friend, partner, or employee or with any other toxic person in your life is a minute you'll never get back and that you could better spend without that person. Do you have any Paytons in your life right now? Hire slow and fire fast. Every minute counts.

FAST First **A**ction **S**teps to **T**ake:

1. Recall two or three people who are no longer in your life whom you perhaps hired too quickly and kept in your life too long. Write down how long you stayed past the point where you knew in your heart you should cut the cord.

2. Evaluate your current employees, partners, and relationships. Are there any people you've met who you know in your gut are not right for you or your organization? If so, begin to make a plan now to fire them as needed.

3. As you think about people you meet, always remember the motto "hire slow, fire fast." Take your time letting them into your inner circle, but don't be afraid to toss them out the second it stops feeling right.

10. Blow Off the Right People

"He's running just a few minutes late, but we'll be right with you," said a well-dressed receptionist at precisely 10:00 A.M. one morning in the lobby of an investment firm I was visiting.

I was so excited! Finally, I was meeting with Brett, a serial entrepreneur turned investor. He had had enormous success at a very young age and was now an active investor in more than three hundred companies with over $1 billion under management. Boy, was I psyched to meet with him. I wasn't sure exactly how I could work with him, but I was confident there would be a way, and so I had worked through a mutual connection over a month before to schedule a meeting. And now here it was, about to happen. We had booked a half hour with his assistant, but secretly I was hoping the conversation would go well and end up taking forty-five minutes to an hour.

"Brett will see you now. Here's a bottle of water; please head on back," said the same lady to me at 10:04 a.m. I thanked her and headed anxiously into Brett's office.

"Great to see you," Brett said warmly but firmly, with his hand out to shake mine. "Tell me a little bit about what you're up to and how I can help."

"Well, given that you're an investor in over three hundred small businesses and we're a software company serving small businesses that also is currently raising money from investors, I thought there would be ample opportunity to partner on something," I replied. I proceeded to give him a quick but high-level view of our software and possible partnership opportunities.

"Okay," Brett said at approximately 10:08 a.m. "You're not an investment opportunity right now because you don't fit our revenue requirement, but you might be a possible partner. Email me a one-sheet when you follow up and I'll have our partnership coordinator take a look. Also, I'm going to introduce you to two people who you should meet who might be mutually beneficial."

He spoke quickly and with confidence. Moreover, as he spoke, Brett was typing away, actually making the introductions via email simultaneously.

"Thanks for coming and all the best, Dave!" Brett exclaimed enthusiastically, sticking his hand back out to shake mine. (It was 10:12 a.m. at this point.)

As I walked out of that office, I was overcome with thoughts. On the one hand, I was tempted to be annoyed that I had had only an eight-minute meeting with this guy I had booked thirty minutes with. On the other hand, during those eight minutes he had been honest, direct, and, most important, extremely helpful in making those introductions and offering me an opportunity to explore a partnership. How could I possibly not be appreciative?

Soon thereafter, my thoughts turned to the incredible skill I had just witnessed. This guy had totally blown me off. (Wouldn't you think "eight minutes of thirty booked after a four-minute lateness" constitutes blowing off?) Yet I walked away not angry at all. In fact, I walked away feeling very appreciative for Brett's time and the value he had provided over that time—all eight minutes of it.

It can be easy to blow people off. You're too busy, and if you're not sure how valuable a person will be, why bother giving him any of your time at all? But it can be even easier to give away your precious time to people who ask for it and then want and take more and more. We all want to be liked, and it's very tempting to give people the time they crave. But if I had had all thirty minutes with Brett, would it really have made a difference? He would have lost twenty-two minutes of productivity, and I probably wouldn't have been any better off. We've all had the experience of trying to get off the phone when the other person keeps talking. It's not fun. You don't want people to feel hurt or blown off, and so it's easier sometimes to give them your time.

That might be the easy thing, but is it the best thing? Or is the best thing to blow people off without having them feel blown off? To guard your most precious asset, your time, ferociously and make sure every minute counts when you are spending it with people? To end a meeting or communication with someone quickly yet have her walk away feeling good about the interaction? These things are hard, but they are worth it. Sheryl Sandberg, the chief operating officer of Facebook, calls it "ruthless prioritization." Let's break down what Brett did to me into three simple steps that you can use to blow off people the right way:

1. Physical interaction (handshake) to indicate both the beginning and the end of the conversation
2. Frank, direct, to-the-point conversation
3. Providing value to the other person before ending the conversation

These three things effectively blew me off and turned a potential thirty-plus minutes of mutually wasted time into eight minutes of mutually beneficial time, leaving twenty-two minutes for each of us to live, work, create, and enjoy.

Using these principles will help you shorten meetings with both the right *and* the wrong people and help you become more productive. It can be relatively easy to use these techniques within the confines of a scheduled meeting or on the home turf of your office. But what about blowing off people who stop you to talk to you in person at unscheduled moments, email you, or text or tweet you? So many people want your time. Some of them are worth it and will help you get what you want; others, frankly, just aren't. Here's a quick guide to the successful blowoff in these less controllable circumstances:

1. **In person: Keep moving.** Once you stop to talk to someone, you start losing valuable time. If you want to keep a conversation short, the best way to do it is to keep walking. You can smile and nod all the way to the elevator, stairs, or wherever it is you're going.
2. **Text/email/tweet: Reply, but as slowly and succinctly as you can.** Sometimes it's hard not to reply right away, but wherever possible, it's important to give the signal that you have other priorities right now. Don't ignore anyone. But when you do reply, whether it's right away or days later, keep your response succinct. I've replied with one-word responses to three-hundred-word emails. If you're positive and helpful, the length of your reply really isn't that important.

We all want to be seen as nice people, and we all want to be liked. But remember, every minute you spend with someone who isn't going to help you get what you want is a minute spent away from someone who *may* help you get what you want. It's also a minute that person is spending with someone who doesn't truly want to be spending it with him. Thus, the right thing to do is to learn the art of the blowoff. Like Brett, you can maximize every minute.

FAST First **A**ction **S**teps to **T**ake:

1. Write down the names of two or three people who typically take up more of your time than you'd like them to at work or in your personal life.
2. Choose one and construct a plan for your next conversation. Plan to quickly define the reason for the conversation, use signals to indicate the start and the end of the conversation, be frank, provide value early on, and end it quickly.
3. Practice artful blowoffs of people who stop you in person to converse as well as people who text, email, and tweet you.

Every minute you spend with **someone** who isn't going to **help you get what you want** is a minute spent away from **someone** who *may* help you get **what you want**.

3

Reading People

11. Stop Waiting to Talk and Start Actually Listening

"Dave, are you even listening to me? Hello? What happened? You just decided to stop listening to me halfway through our date?"

We were on our first date, and Robin, a twenty-one-year-old beautiful brunette, was not happy. She was not wrong, either. Well, not completely wrong, anyway. I didn't actively decide to stop listening to her, but I might as well have, as I had effectively lost my ability to pay attention, a fact that clearly had not escaped her.

This was a first date gone horribly wrong. And when I say first date, I mean it literally. Yes, embarrassing but true, my first date didn't occur until I was a twenty-one-year-old college senior. Anyway, I finally had gotten the courage to ask this girl from my classes out, and much to my excitement, she had said yes. That Friday night, I was excited to enjoy drinks and dinner with Robin at one of the nicest restaurants on Boylston Street in Boston. I psyched myself up, thought of my best stories to tell, and tried to remember the advice my best friend had given me: Make sure to listen to her.

But once the date actually began, I was way too nervous to follow the playbook I had prepared. At first, I did a great job listening—so great, in fact, that seventeen years later I still recall Robin's goals and her classes for that semester. But at some point during the date (perhaps after the second drink) I went into storytelling mode. I had so many interesting stories prepared, and I figured surely she would be impressed and entertained by them.

The problem was that as soon as I finished telling a story, I completely tuned out her reply. Not because I didn't care about what she had to say but because I was preoccupied thinking of the next story I would tell. And thinking about how the date was going. And thinking about what I was going to do to transition the date to its next location after dinner. And all that thinking about what to say next kept me from executing the single most important part of reading people and communicating well: listening.

In this I was not alone. In fact, most of the time people aren't really listening to you; they're waiting to talk. They are thinking about what's next, or what to say, or almost anything else but what the person in front of them is saying. The thing about listening is that it requires a relentless focus that most people don't have or don't use.

The *Merriam-Webster Dictionary* defines listening as "hearing something with thoughtful attention: giving consideration." In other words, listening is clearly more than just hearing. It is the act of consciously paying attention to someone else in an attempt to understand, to consider. It is the process of thinking about what is important to someone else rather than what may be important to you. It is the act at any given moment of caring more about what someone else has to say than anything else in the world. Listening is hard—a lot harder than you might think.

Before we can learn how to read and understand people, it's essential to be able to listen to them. In fact, I would go so far as to say that if there's just one people skill you take away from this book, it should be listening. Dr. Gerald D. Bell, founder and CEO of Bell Leadership Institute and a professor at the University of North Carolina's Kenan-Flagler Business School, has over forty years of experience working with top business leaders. He has seen firsthand the impact great listening skills have. Says Bell, "When you listen to people, they feel valued, respected, happy, and productive. They feel more motivated, inspired, and eager to solve problems and produce good results." He also notes the damaging effects of poor listening skills: "When we don't listen to people, they feel hurt, rejected, demeaned, disrespected, and de-motivated." Simply put, listening skills can make or break any interaction in business or in personal relationships.

After conducting years of research on the most effective and least effective traits of leaders, Bell advised leaders to "listen like children watch TV." Think about that. Children sit up straight, slightly leaning in to the TV. Their eyes are glued to the screen. Bell calls it the Achiever Listening position and recommends it as a first step in improving one's listening skills.

The idea is to imagine you're glued to the TV screen, except the TV screen is the person in front of you. It helps to lean in and have your arms at your side, and whenever your mind wanders away from what the person is saying (all of our minds wander, so that's okay), refocus on listening for understanding. Again, you're not listening with intent to respond, or listening with intent to talk, or listening with intent to do anything but understand what the person is saying and why. The rest will follow.

After Robin called me out for not listening, I snapped back to attention, but it was only momentary. Sadly, I wasn't ready to be a good listener back then, or a good date for that matter, and that date with Robin was both the first and the last. But I have since learned to do much better by following the simple rules below. Now, you can do better, too. (You can visit the Bell Leadership Institute at BellArtofPeople.com.)

FAST First Action Steps to Take:

1. Practice the Achiever Listening position. Have a conversation with someone during which you are distinctly focused on achieving optimal understanding. Don't think about what you are going to say next or do next. Just focus solely on what she is saying.

2. Watch someone (preferably a child) watching television. Note his rapt concentration on the screen in front of him. This is what you want when you are listening.
3. Remember that listening is a lifetime activity and that we all can continuously improve this essential skill. Take at least a half hour every month to get completely silent in a meeting and practice active listening.

12. Words Mean Little; Listen with Your Eyes, Not Your Ears

I've got it!" I said to my boss, Peggy, who had just trained me in how to be better at listening. I was a salesperson for Disney at the time, and I wanted to learn anything I could to sell more advertising. "I will pay attention to exactly what words come out of the mouths of any prospects I'm meeting with. This is going to be great!"

'Well, there is one more thing," Peggy replied. "Actually, there's something much more important than the words that come out of a prospect's mouth that you've got to pay attention to."

"What could be more important than what they're saying?" I asked dubiously.

"More important than what they're saying is how they're saying it," Peggy answered.

As it turns out, Peggy was completely correct: Way more important than listening to the words people are saying is listening to the tone of their voice and reading their so-called body language, or gestures. In fact, research has shown that 93 percent of communication is non-verbal!

According to landmark research conducted by Albert Mehrabian, Susan Ferris, and Morton Wiener in 1967, body language is responsible for 55 percent of what is communicated, tone for 38 percent, and language for only 7 percent. Although some quibble about the numbers and the 55/38/7 formula has been debated, what's not debated is the overall importance of body language for reading and understanding others.

Thus, when you're listening to people, it's not enough just to hear their words; you need to read their body language as well. By this I don't mean obvious gestures such as a frown or an eye roll. There are many different types of nonverbal communication. Here is a brief guide to the nonverbal signals and cues that people use and what they communicate. In general, the more you practice reading people for understanding, the better you'll get at it.

Facial expressions

The human face is extremely expressive, able to convey countless emotions without a word being said. Unlike some forms of nonverbal communication, facial expressions are universal. The facial expressions for happiness, sadness, anger, surprise, fear, and disgust are the same across cultures. Look closely at people's facial expressions as they speak. Are their brows raised to indicate anger or discomfort? Are their faces lit up with enthusiasm or wrinkled with exhaustion? Each little cue gives you a better understanding and a potential advantage.

Body movements and posture

The way people sit, walk, stand, hold their heads, move, and carry themselves communicates a wealth of information to the world. This type of nonverbal communication includes posture, bearing, stance, and subtle movements. Does the person you're speaking with look comfortable or uncomfortable in her posture? Figuring out the answer to this question goes a long way toward understanding the individual and her circumstances. A comfortable stance could indicate openness and flexibility, whereas a more uncomfortable stance might indicate closed-mindedness or anxiety.

Gestures

Gestures are woven into the fabric of our daily lives. We wave, point, beckon, and use our hands when we're arguing or speaking animatedly, expressing ourselves with gestures often without thinking about it. However, the meaning of gestures can be very different across cultures and regions, and so it's important to be careful to avoid misinterpretation. One classic gesture is crossing one's arms; in most Western cultures, this can mean anger or discomfort. Similarly, in these cultures, constantly touching one's face while speaking can indicate discomfort or a lie.

Eye contact

Since the visual sense is dominant for most people, eye contact is an especially important type of nonverbal communication. The way someone looks at you can communicate many things, including interest, affection, hostility, and attraction. It is easier to establish rapport with someone who's willing to make solid eye contact with you. Eye contact is also important in maintaining the flow of conversation and gauging the other person's response.

Touch

We communicate a great deal through touch. Think about the messages given by the following: a weak handshake, a timid tap on the shoulder, a warm bear hug, a reassuring slap on the back, a patronizing pat on the head, and a controlling grip on the arm. Pay attention to how you're touched at the beginning of a conversation.

Space

Have you ever felt uncomfortable during a conversation because the other person was standing too close and invading your space? We all have a need for physical space, although that need differs with the culture, the situation, and the closeness of the relationship. You can use physical space to communicate many different nonverbal messages, including signals of intimacy and affection, aggression, or dominance. For example, a "close talker" might have issues of aggression or a lack of self-esteem that is being overcompensated for by the closeness.

Voice

It's not just what you say, it's *how* you say it. When people speak, you can "read" their voices in addition to their body language. Things to pay attention to include timing and pace, how loudly they're speaking, tone and inflection, and sounds that convey understanding, such as "ahh" and "uh-huh." Think about how someone's tone of voice can indicate sarcasm, anger, affection, or confidence.

Ultimately, becoming a better reader of body language is all about paying attention and practicing. By paying attention to facial expressions, posture, gestures, eye contact, touch, space, and voice during conversations, you'll be able to read people and understand what they're thinking, feeling, and trying to convey better than you could yesterday. You'll notice when people have good intentions and when they're hiding something, when people are nervous and when people are confident, when people are comfortable and when they're not so comfortable. All of this intelligence will help you to listen to, and persuade, people better.

I took in all this advice from Peggy and in time became not only a better listener but a better people reader as well. After all, up to 93 percent of my ability to listen well depends on it!

FAST First **A**ction **S**teps to **T**ake:

1. Practice reading people's body language. Have a conversation with a close friend or family member during which you are distinctly focused on achieving optimal understanding by observing that person's body language. Note her facial

expressions, movements, gestures, and so on, and try to guess what they communicate about her thoughts and intentions.

2. After the conversation, circle back and share your observations and ask the person whether your assumptions were correct. Check to see how well you read that person.

3. Remember that as much as 93 percent of listening consists of paying attention to body language and tone. Paying attention to the words is just a start to becoming a better listener.

13. Always Accept the Glass of Water

"Oh, no thanks," I said to Sue, the marketing director for a major bank in Boston I was about to pitch on a sales call, in response to her offer of coffee or water. "I don't want to be a bother," I thought to myself. I was running a couple of minutes late, and I wanted to make the most of our time, so I passed on a cold drink of water that I actually craved.

But I was really thirsty. And that got me to thinking that maybe I should have taken the water. It was hot in that room, I realized. I was nervous about the meeting, too, as it was a big pitch. Nervousness plus the warmth of the room led to some sweat, and now I wanted that glass of water more than ever.

As anyone who's ever been in sales or ever presented for business knows, once you start sweating, it's simply a bad, bad situation. Now I was so worried that Sue would notice I was sweating profusely, I lost focus on what I was there to do. As you can imagine, Sue's meeting with sweaty Dave didn't go very well, and it all started with my saying no to water to keep from being a bother.

You surely have had the experience of going somewhere for an interview or meeting and being offered water, coffee, tea, or soda. You may have thought the same thing I thought that day: Don't be a bother.

After that disaster of a meeting with Sue, though, I decided to do an unscientific study. At my next twenty meetings, I alternated between taking the water (or whatever the other party offered) and politely saying no. Then I compared the results of each meeting.

As it turns out, it's best to be a bother if that means taking the coffee, soda, or water you're offered. The meetings at which I took the offer went significantly better than did the ones at which I didn't. I know, small sample size and totally unscientific study, but it makes sense, doesn't it?

In doing this experiment I learned that there are two reasons taking the drink sets you up for success. First, it puts you at ease and allows you to relax, cool off, or warm up and get ready for the meeting. Second and more important, it puts the other person at ease.

Think about when you have people over to your home. I'm sure you offer them water or a drink or a snack, and typically they take it. When they don't, it throws you off: "Why won't this person take my drink or snack?" you think. "Am I a terrible host?" "What's the deal?" Your mind may wander, and now you're distracted and maybe even annoyed at your guest for putting you in that situation.

When the tables are turned and you're offered a drink at the start of a meeting, take it. Even if you're not thirsty, take the drink. If you're offered coffee and you don't drink coffee, politely ask for water instead. This very simple act will make the person you're meeting with feel like a good host, put him at ease, and prime you to be able to read him well and exert influence as needed.

Remember, being liked is all about making people feel good, and accepting a drink allows the other person to feel good. Two quick caveats about this approach: First, if you're not offered a beverage, don't ask for one; that could easily have the opposite effect, making the other person feel bad that she doesn't have anything to offer. Second, when food is offered, unless you're actually having a lunch meeting, it's best to decline politely. Food is simply too distracting when you want to be at your best.

By the way, ever since I completed that study, I always accept a beverage at every meeting. It's usually water, but I've had my share of soda, juice, and even the occasional beer and wine to kick off a meeting. Cheers!

FAST First **A**ction **S**teps to **T**ake:

1. Commit to accepting a beverage at all your meetings and interviews.
2. Be sure to offer one whenever possible when people are meeting you at your office.
3. When you are waiting for the beverage, use the opportunity to settle in, relax, and set up for success mentally and physically.

14. Bluffing Is Only for Poker

"Look, I want to hire you," Charlie, an older mustached Greek-American, said to me from across the table in his restaurant. "I really do. It's just that I can't afford you for $500 a month. If you can't lower your price, I'm going to have to go with my cousin, who will help me for just a couple hundred dollars a month."

As he said that last sentence, he scratched his face a couple of times and looked away from me—one of the surest signs of lying or at least discomfort (see Chapter 12)—and I determined that he was bluffing. I was just getting started as a consultant at that time, and though I really wanted the money, most of our clients were paying between $2,000 and $3,000 a month, and so I already was giving Charlie an amazing deal. Sure, I could come down on the price to meet what he was asking for, but I was trying to build a business, and sometimes walking away is the right thing to do in a situation like this.

"Charlie, I would love to work with you, too," I replied. "I really would. But I'm afraid I just can't go below $500 a month. I hope you'll change your mind and work with us, and I think that if you do, you'll be very happy. But if not, I wish you and your cousin the best of luck in your marketing work."

It was hard to call his bluff, because I really did want him as a client. But as it turned out, my instinct was the right one.

"You know what, Dave?" Charlie replied. "I'm going to give you a shot. I think you're expensive, but I think you're worth it."

Here's what I learned from this experience: Everywhere except the poker table, bluffing fails. In poker, the game is designed to give bluffers a chance. You can take a calculated risk, and sometimes it pays off, and your opponent never knows if you were bluffing. But in the game of life, bluffing is simply too risky. On the upside, bluffing can help you persuade people to work for you for less (or more) than you want, or pay more money for something you have to offer, or help you achieve another goal. I could have given in to Charlie's bluff, for instance, and he could have saved a few bucks. But on the downside, bluffing erodes trust. A bluffer is not being authentic in his or her actions, and if he or she is called on it, that becomes apparent and the long-term relationship is damaged. After that one interaction, I never could take Charlie's words at face value, because I always wondered if he was bluffing again.

However, the fact is that just because you and I know that bluffing works only in poker, that doesn't mean that everyone you do business with knows it. In fact, bluffs are pretty common in business, and a key skill for reading and understanding people is learning to detect them.

The best poker players in the world are masters at reading body language and tone. They know how to interpret even the slightest differences in gestures, and as soon as they can sense discomfort (in poker it's called a tell), they know how and when to pounce and call the bluff.

Even if you're not a card player, you can use the same techniques to your advantage. Watch closely when you're having a conversation that involves a negotiation or sale. The first thing to read and understand is your conversation partner's baseline: how he acts when *not* under pressure. Then, as the conversation gets deeper and the moment of truth arrives ("So, are you able to move forward now at this price?"), look for shifts in appearance or tone as he's talking.

Scratching his face? Could be bluffing.

Fidgeting more than before? Could be bluffing.

Speeding up the pace of talking? Could be bluffing.

Now, of course, this person might *not* be bluffing in these situations. He might just be uncomfortable. But even if you're not 100 percent or even 50 percent sure he's bluffing, you should still call him on it, because if he is bluffing and you call it successfully, you'll not only save that much more time, money, and peace of mind, you'll gain valuable information about how trustworthy this person is and in turn how valuable he is to you as a client, a colleague, or a business partner.

Charlie and I went on to work together for over a year at $500 a month until I fired him as a client and moved on. I told him at the time that I had to charge him $1,000 a month or I couldn't afford to service him anymore. He thought I was bluffing. I wasn't. But that's another story.

FAST First **A**ction **S**teps to **T**ake:

1. Practice reading people to determine whether they're bluffing. It's great to have a partner to do this with and even a deck of cards. Obviously, poker is one way to practice, but even if you don't play poker, simply have your partner hold up a card so that you can't see it, tell you what that card is, and have you predict whether she's telling the truth. Over time, you'll get better at reading your partner's tells and body language and get more accurate at calling bluffs.
2. Begin to notice body language and possible tells in the people you interact with on a regular basis at work and at home.
3. Don't bluff yourself! Authenticity and transparency are more powerful and persuasive than any bluff.

15. The One Trick That Seems Ridiculous but Works Every Time

"This is stupid and a total waste of my time!"

I didn't say that, but boy, was I thinking it. I had taken an entire day off from work for this group I had just joined called the Entrepreneurs' Organization. I was excited to join this forum of seven to nine CEOs whom I'd meet with on a monthly basis, but I had to be trained first. So here I was attending "Forum Training" with seven other entrepreneurs, where I had just been taught about something called mirroring.

Mirroring, we were told, means repeating back exactly something that someone else in the forum said, word for word, preceded by "I hear you saying" or "I heard you say." For example, if I heard a forum member say, "I'm feeling worried about losing our biggest client," I would mirror that person by replying: "I hear you saying you're feeling worried about losing your biggest client."

In those few minutes after we were taught how to mirror and began practicing it, I was cynical. I had just spent thousands of dollars to join this organization and had taken an entire precious day off from work to attend this training, and I felt like I was back in kindergarten. What good could saying the exact words back to someone possibly do? It seemed frivolous, fake, and, well, stupid.

Then it was my turn to be mirrored, and everything changed.

I talked for several minutes about pretty deep stuff from my past—my father's mental illness, my unrequited love for a married woman, my struggles with weight—and the feelings associated with those issues. Afterward, we went around the table, and each person mirrored me by repeating one thing he or she heard me say:

"I heard you say you've struggled all of your life with weight and that it feels like a constant battle."

"I heard you saying you've had to deal with your dad's bipolar disorder for over twenty years and that sometimes it feels really lonely."

"I heard you say you were in love with a married woman and that felt impossible at the time but that eventually you let her go, and then you ended up together, and that felt amazing."

"Wow," I thought. I felt heard. I felt listened to. I felt that they really cared about me. I had just met these people that morning, and I felt so close to them. It was the power of mirroring, and it felt amazing. My feelings about mirroring changed forever.

As it turns out, mirroring is a massively powerful concept that allows you to connect deeply to people. It's easier said than done, however. Simply repeating back what you're hearing can help you forge a bond with other people and win their trust, but it also can be interpreted as insincere and inauthentic. There's only one very simple solution to this: *You have to actually care about what you're mirroring.*

If you repeat back out loud what you're hearing in a robotic monotone, people are not going to believe you actually care about what they are saying. But if you repeat it back with emotion, with an emphasis on the important words and feelings that were just spoken, you give it meaning. You help the other person feel heard and listened to. You demonstrate that you care.

People in general don't want advice even when they ask for it. They just want to feel heard. As you practice and get good at mirroring, you will help people feel heard, and they will love you for it. Focus on really emphasizing the "feeling words" you hear as well; mirroring feelings is much more valuable than mirroring thoughts.

People don't want **advice** even when they **ask for it**. They just want to **feel heard**.

Of course, the greater the emotional depth of the conversation is, the more powerful the mirroring can be. If someone says, "I'm feeling okay. Took the kids to school and did some laundry," simply mirroring back "I hear you say you're feeling okay after taking the kids to school and doing some laundry" won't make as big an impact as mirroring a deeper statement would. Even so, as ridiculous as it seemed to me at first and as ridiculous as you may think it is, mirroring is an incredible tool for connecting with others.

One caveat: Don't bungle their words. Remember, the reason mirroring is so powerful is that the person being mirrored feels totally heard. If she says, "I'm upset over the work that you did; it's sloppy," and you reply with "I hear you; you're angry with me over poorly done work," it's not quite the same, and rather than feeling heard, she will feel that you weren't listening carefully. Therefore, it's essential to keep practicing those listening skills in order to mirror well.

One more caveat: Never use the word *but* after a mirroring statement. Imagine you're angry because your husband said he would take out the garbage and forgot to do it. Then imagine saying to him, "I'm angry because you said you'd take the garbage out and you didn't," and him replying, "I hear you. You're angry that I said I would take the garbage out and didn't." Now imagine that he adds, "But I've been really busy with work stuff, and it just slipped my mind." His attempt at mirroring has been ruined by just one word. No *but*s.

Five years after that forum training, I still meet with my EO forum every single month, and we share updates on our lives and mirror one another. My seven forum mates have become my closest friends in the world, and I owe a great debt of gratitude to that "stupid" training in mirroring.

FAST First Action Steps to Take:

1. Practice mirroring with a trusted friend or close colleague. Sit face-to-face and have your partner share how he's doing, including his highs and lows of recent weeks and the feelings associated with those events. After a few minutes, share a couple of mirroring statements that are based on what you heard. Ask your partner how well you did. Then switch roles. It feels great to be mirrored, too.
2. Experiment with using mirroring in situations in which someone is upset. At work, this might include customer service, sales, or any disagreement. At home, this might mean an argument with your boyfriend or wife. Remember to focus on repeating back the feelings and what you heard word for word.
3. As you get better at mirroring, you'll find that people respond to you more and more. You'll sharpen your listening skills and help everyone in your life feel heard. They'll all remember you as the one who gets them, the one who really cares.

4

Connecting with People

16. Validate, Validate, Validate

Boy, was I angry! I had just been on hold for over forty-five minutes on the phone with my cable TV company to fix a billing error, and a minute into the conversation, after I had waited so long to talk to a human being, the call had been disconnected. Now I was waiting for another thirty minutes in a new queue to talk to a human being. I was angry, I was frustrated, I was fed up! Finally, someone answered.

Afraid of getting disconnected and kicked back to the end of the line again, I responded to the representative's greeting with "Hi, this is Dave. I've been waiting for over an hour on two separate calls. Got disconnected, so if we get disconnected again, please please please call me back at 617-905-XXXX. In the meantime, I need your help, please, because my bill is over $250 more than it should be!" I was trying to stay calm, but my voice betrayed that I was angry.

"Wow," the lady on the other end of the phone said in disbelief.

"I hear you saying you've been waiting for over an hour to talk with us," she continued, "and that your bill is over $250 more than it should be. You must be so angry and frustrated!"

I could actually hear *her* on the other end of the line getting angry with her own company and with what was happening to me.

"Yeah, I'm angry and frustrated," I replied with enthusiasm.

"Man, I would be so angry if that happened to me," she continued. "I'll tell you what; let me get all of your information and let's see if we can get this sorted out. And if we get disconnected for any reason, I'll call you right back, that's for sure. Boy, I hate when these problems happen to me, and I'm a customer, too. My name is Maureen, by the way, Dave."

Then a very curious thing happened. Almost immediately, I wasn't that angry anymore. It was as if my anger and frustration had lifted in a cloud of understanding and camaraderie. I felt heard. I felt surprised. I felt vindicated. And she hadn't even fixed my problem yet!

The next few minutes were nothing short of delightful. I took Maureen through the billing error, which was in fact the company's fault. Maureen then credited the entire $256-plus discrepancy back to my account and, to put icing on the cake, credited my account an additional $100 to "make up for your troubles."

"Thank you so much, Maureen," I said sincerely. I had gotten a much better, faster resolution than I'd expected and had only her to thank.

"Well, you're welcome," Maureen replied. "It feels good to have something frustrating like this resolved quickly and to your liking, doesn't it?"

It was the best customer service I'd ever had, and as I hung up the phone, I realized my mood had shifted from fury and frustration to feeling good about life. I was even feeling positive about the dreaded cable company.

Why had my mood shifted so fast and so dramatically? Obviously, the fact that my billing issue was (eventually) solved quickly was a contributing factor. But it was more than that. I had had my feelings validated by Maureen; that validation was what made me feel so much better. It was as if I could no longer be angry with her because now she was on my team. Maureen not only had heard me, she'd actually *felt me*. She had put herself in my shoes and had shown me that she totally understood how I felt by feeling my emotions with me. It was empathy. It was mirroring. It was validation. It was great!

Mirroring is a great way to help people feel heard, but *validation* takes mirroring to a whole new level. The idea is to put yourself in the other person's shoes and, in addition to repeating back exactly what she has said, say something to suggest you understand how she *probably* is feeling. You can even try to feel those emotions yourself, as Maureen did that day. If this is done well, the effect of validation is extremely powerful: You can diffuse negative emotions, get harmony around positive emotions, and build strong, long-lasting connections in just a few short minutes, as Maureen did with me.

Just one caveat: There is a major risk to validation that doesn't exist with mirroring. In mirroring, you're saying *exactly* what you heard. Listen well and you can't go wrong. In validating, you're *interpreting* the feelings you *think* you're hearing. Interpret wrong and you can totally miss and have the opposite effect to what you want: Instead of deeply connecting, you are confusing the situation.

The solution is that if you're unsure of the feeling associated with what you're hearing, keep listening and asking questions. You can validate more tentatively as well, taking cues from the other person's reactions. For instance, if you think the emotion you're hearing is anger, you might say, "Sounds like you're pretty angry, eh?" as a question. You'll get either "Yeah, I'm angry!" as a reply or "Not really. More like frustrated." Either way, you'll have the clarification you need to get it right.

Validation is the single most powerful way of connecting with other people. Sure, it can be difficult to validate if you don't agree with the person you're validating or if you feel differently. But remember, validation is not agreement; it's not giving in, giving up, or admitting you're wrong. It's just showing the other person that you understand where she's coming from and genuinely care. Even if there is a disagreement, instead of getting defensive (which is what most people do), you'll have a much better chance of a happy resolution if you validate the other person's feelings and have her feel more connected to you.

Sadly, most customer-service calls to utility companies don't go the way my call with Maureen did, but imagine if they did!

FAST First Action Steps to Take:

1. Listen for "feeling" words and expressions as you have conversations. Pay attention to body language and tone as well when you are face-to-face. Practice replying with a validation statement such as "You must feel . . ."
2. Practice validation with a friend who knows what you're doing. Ask if your validation statements were accurate reflections of how he was in fact feeling and whether they made a difference in the way he feels.
3. One of the challenges of validation is that with more practice and as you get better at it, it can appear less genuine. Remember to be sincere in all your validation statements. That sincerity (or insincerity) does show.

17. The Most Important Question You'll Ever Ask in a First Meeting

"So what's your question?"

Two years ago, Michael Kislin, a financial adviser I had met at an event I had spoken at, met with me for the first time in my offices. I get solicited a lot for meetings with financial advisers and commercial real estate professionals, and so my guard is always up when they ask to meet with me. But Michael seemed like a nice enough guy and promised that he wouldn't take more than fifteen minutes, that he had just one real question for me, and that he wouldn't try to sell me anything. It seemed like an offer I couldn't refuse.

Still, when it came time to meet and he sat down in front of me, I was nervous. Would he somehow try to sneakily sell me? What did he want from me? And what was this mysterious one question he wanted to ask me? We exchanged small talk, and he told me a little about his business. He was establishing a niche as a financial adviser to tech start-up entrepreneurs. Although many of his clients weren't wealthy yet, his idea was to build relationships with them all now so that as some of them did succeed and amass wealth, he'd be there to help them (and make money, of course). Then the moment of truth came. I asked Michael what his one big question was, and he replied: "How can I help you?"

Frankly, I wasn't sure at first how he could help me. But then I had an idea. I told him about my latest start-up venture, Likeable Local, and said I could use some introductions to early-stage technology investors. He asked me a bunch of questions to learn more about the specifics of whom I was looking to reach. Then we wrapped up the conversation, and he said he'd be in touch, but only if it was with something that could be helpful. No sales pitch. No gimmicks. Michael just sincerely promised to follow up if and only if he could actually help me. And that he did.

The next week, Michael introduced me via email to three different early-stage tech investors he thought I would want to meet. Although I didn't end up taking investment money from any of those three individuals, I did genuinely feel very grateful to Michael. As a result, when I called to thank him, I asked him to tell me more about what he did. As he told me about his business, it dawned on me that I did have a need for a financial adviser. I soon became a client of Michael's, and my wife and I have been working with him ever since. He didn't try to sell me, he didn't try to persuade me, and he didn't try to trick me. The idea to hire him had not been his but mine. All because of one question.

My father-in-law, the Honorable Steven Fisher, always taught me to "show your friendship first." What he meant by that is that you should show the other party you're there to help him, that you care, before you even consider asking something of him in return. There's no better way to show that you care about the person you're meeting with than to genuinely, authentically ask her what you can do to help.

There are two possibilities for what can happen when you ask, "How can I help you?":

1. The person will tell you, giving you an opportunity to help, after which he will feel indebted to you, connected to you, and appreciative of you, and will eventually feel compelled to return the favor and help *you* one day.
2. The person will decline politely, probably because she doesn't know how you can help her, but will feel that you care and feel connected to you and be much more emotionally invested in helping you eventually, even if you never have to lift a finger for her.

Either way, by establishing that you care and that you're there to help, you'll gain trust and eventually influence. So, the most important question you'll ever ask is: "How can I help you?"

The most **important question** you'll ever ask: **"How can I help you?"**

If it seems simple, that's because it is. It doesn't matter whether it's a customer, a prospect, or a colleague you're meeting with: We all like to be cared about, and we all can use some help. Just make sure you're genuine and never contrived or inauthentic when you ask, and of course be sure to follow through on anything you promise or commit to. Also, ideally, make sure the other person knows a little about you and your network, expertise, and sphere of influence so that when you ask him how you can help, you are fully equipped with the tools to provide any help he asks for. You also should do your research about the other party so that you know, going in, various ways you could help. One of the greatest ways to help people is to introduce them to other people (more on that later).

The best part about "How can I help you?" is the long-lasting effects of that one simple question. Case in point: Not only am I *still* a happy client of Michael Kislin's, I appreciate his ability to show his friendship first so much that I've introduced him to several people who have become his clients. I hope that's just the beginning of the ways I can help him.

FAST **F**irst **A**ction **S**teps to **T**ake:

1. Practice asking "How can I help you?" with a friend before trying it out on a new person in your life. Get comfortable describing your sphere of influence and expertise and then practice asking the question sincerely.
2. Try this out with a new person you meet with in a professional setting. Make sure your offer to help is authentic, and agree to do only things on which you can actually deliver.
3. Go to people you already know and set up meetings to offer to help them as well. You'll be surprised how much more deeply and better you'll connect with people when you do this.

18. Who You Are Online Is Who You Are in Life

The birth of our company may have been a dream, but there were days, weeks, and even months early on that felt more like a nightmare. We couldn't get a loan from a bank. We couldn't hire the right people. We couldn't manage our cash flow very well. We nearly missed payroll several times. We brought arguments from home to work, and we brought arguments from work to home."

When I wrote those words in a blog post and shared it on LinkedIn, Twitter, and Facebook, it was four years into the start of our first company. We had a growing staff of about twenty employees, and I remember one of our management team members approaching me just after I published the post. She said, "Dave, don't you think the post is a little, well, raw? Do you really want potential clients seeing how close we were to going under? Don't you think it might turn people off to share so personally about your business?"

I thought about it a bit and then replied, "You could very well be right. Let's call them up and ask them."

We called a few of our larger clients, sent them the post, and asked for their feedback. I was getting nervous. Although intuitively I believed that we'd be fine, my employee's concern had me increasingly worried. Then an email from our largest client came in.

"Wow, this is great," it read. "Do you mind if I share the article with other people?"

"Of course!" I replied. "That's what it's there for. Feel free to share, and thanks for your feedback."

The positive feedback continued as more and more emails began to roll in. It seemed that our current clients didn't have any problem with my candid description of the company's rocky start. But then something happened that really surprised me.

We got a referral. A new, major client.

"I'd like to set up a call to talk about a new project we'd like your help on," the email read. "I appreciated your honesty and vulnerability in the article your client Elana forwarded to me. Look forward to talking."

Unbelievable! Not only had we not upset our clients with that honest, vulnerable piece, we actually had attracted a new client. I went back to the employee who had shown concern that the post would have the opposite effect.

"Thank you for being honest with me about your concern," I said. "So what do you think ended up working about the piece?"

"It was risky," she replied. "But that's the whole thing. By taking a risk and sharing your true thoughts and feelings, you connected with people at a deeper level, and that's exactly what worked. Authenticity. Even vulnerability," she concluded.

She was right. As it turns out, as scary and impersonal as the Internet and blogging may feel, it's your ability to be your honest, vulnerable, unique self that provides the biggest opportunity to stand out. There are over 100 million blogs in the world, but there's just one that has the distinct, unique voice that you have: yours.

Could it have gone the other way? Could people have been turned off by that blog post and chosen not to do business with us? Of course. (Heck, that may have happened. I'll never know.)

But the bottom line is that that post reflected the real me for better or for worse, and I probably wouldn't have wanted to work with customers who couldn't appreciate me for who I was, anyway.

That brings me to the larger point: Who you are online is who you are in life and vice versa. There is no need to have a different writing style for your professional blog, a different voice for your professional Twitter feed, or separate social media profiles for your personal life and your professional life. Why? Because "business you" and "personal you" are the exact same person. Or they can be. Otherwise, you're going to find yourself trying to manage split personalities and double lives, which is tiring, unnecessary, and ineffective. Imagine logging in and out of different Facebook profiles all day, for instance, to keep up a Chinese wall between personal friends and work friends. Or every time you feel like sending a tweet having to double-check which account you're tweeting from. Too difficult, I say. It's much easier to be the authentic you all the time.

Some people have two very public personalities; others prefer to keep semiprivate online identities, carefully curating their digital selves and handpicking who sees what. But those aren't their actual identities; those are masks they wear, and they aren't fooling anyone.

Most business books and career counselors will advise you to guard tightly anything personal about yourself online for fear that it will be seen by potential employers or recruiters and harm your professional prospects. But let's be serious: We all have our lives outside work, and if I'm hiring someone, I want to see that he's a real person, with friends and family and a personal life; otherwise the only two conclusions are that that person is a robot or that she has something to hide. I'd go so far as to say that if two equally qualified job applicants were placed in front of me, one with a completely open Facebook profile with drunk photos displayed for the whole world to see and the other with a blocked account, I would choose the open one. The type of person I want working for me is the type of person who is willing to share her true self with others.

That means people like Aliza Licht, author and longtime senior vice president of global communications at Donna Karan New York, who is exactly the same online as she is in real life. With hundreds of thousands of Twitter followers, she still considers each member of her audience a friend, reading all tweets and responding to most consistently in her own voice. Her Twitter feed offers an honest glimpse into her life and career, sharing photos from shoots, personal anecdotes, and thoughtful advice. And she doesn't draw the line between her career and her personal life. This practice has allowed her to rise to the top of the public relations industry and gained DKNY a winning reputation for its connectedness to its customers and the customers' brand loyalty.

Social media provide a great opportunity to display authenticity and gain credibility, particularly for business leaders. In fact, in a recent survey, 82 percent of the respondents reported that they are more likely to trust a brand when the senior leadership and CEO are using social media. Today's connected consumers look to social media to determine who companies are and what they stand for. But just being on social media isn't enough; you must use those channels correctly, and that starts with being authentically who you are.

Dennis Crowley, cofounder and CEO of the location-based social network Foursquare, is a prime example. An employee of mine once checked into Foursquare from her favorite trivia night bar on the Lower East Side of Manhattan, and in her tweet to @Dens (his Twitter handle) gave Crowley a shout-out for fixing the Foursquare servers, which had been down earlier that day. Not only did Crowley respond to her personally, he mentioned that he lived in the area, recommended a few other bars for her trivia team to check out, and even gave her his address (around Eighth Street and Avenue B in case you're curious). Although I'm certainly not recommending that you tweet your Social Security number, Crowley's demonstration of trust and openness holds a valuable lesson: When you reveal personal information, you instantly become personable.

As you develop your online persona, be sure to convey your in-real-life self in your digital presence. Rather than trying to create boundaries between personal and professional and online and offline, learn to harmonize them. Find and share your authentic voice.

Years later, I still write about and share the good times and the bad online. It may not always be pretty, but it's always real, and the world will always appreciate the real you.

FAST First **A**ction **S**teps to **T**ake:

1. Write down a list of your online social profiles: social networks, blogs, anywhere you appear online. Do an "authenticity audit": Look at each profile and determine how authentic and vulnerable you're being on it.
2. Think about how you can increase your authenticity and experiment with sharing more of your real self online.
3. Write down a story about a mistake you once made and the lesson you learned from it. Consider posting it on your Facebook wall, your blog, or LinkedIn.

19. Crying Is for Winners

"Crying is for losers," Jamaal teased. Sixth grade was a tough school year for me. As a member of what the bullies called the nerd herd, I often was teased for being unpopular or for being overweight. In this particular incident, I was being socially tortured because word had gotten out that I had a crush on a girl named Deirdre and that when Deirdre found out, she said, "That's disgusting. I wouldn't kiss David if he were the last boy on earth."

Naturally I was crushed by this news, as any twelve-year-old boy would be, but it got worse when I was made fun of for crying by the cool kids, led by Jamaal. "Loser," he said. "Only a fat loser would cry about a girl. Crying is for losers."

That incident stayed with me for many years, as did my belief in his words.

But at our first management retreat, six years ago, my attitude changed overnight. I had gathered five members of the Likeable Media executive team at Foxwoods, a resort and casino in Connecticut, between our New York and Boston offices. The retreat was our first opportunity to get away from the office and plan the company's strategy for the future. I also saw it as an opportunity to connect more deeply with our leadership team. With my wife as our chief operating officer at the time, I obviously was connected on a very deep level with her. But how connected could the rest of our small leadership team get? I wasn't sure what to expect, but I hoped to facilitate a two-day session that would bring us all closer together.

To that end, after setting the tone by asking for confidentiality, I began the first evening session with a quick two minutes of silence to help us focus. Then I asked all the participants to share the most difficult experiences they'd ever had and what they had learned from them. I said that I would set an example for what I expected by going first.

I began to talk about my dad's mental illness when I was a kid and how profoundly it had affected me. I talked about ambulances, shaved heads, and running and screaming in the street. The details of that story aren't important here. What is important is that as I began to share my profound sadness about how my father's chronic condition shaped my childhood, I began to cry. As I started crying, the inner voice in my head told me, "Crying is for losers." But I couldn't stop. I felt embarrassed and even a little ashamed for crying in front of our entire executive team, but the tears just kept coming.

But then a curious thing happened. As we went around the room, as each person shared the most difficult experience of his or her life and spoke with intense emotional depth and vulnerability, I was suddenly not the only one crying. In fact, three of the five people in our group besides me cried as well. By the end of the session, though our faces were wet and we were emotionally exhausted, we were superconnected as a group. It was downright amazing. One executive even said to me, "This is crazy. I feel closer to you guys right now than I feel to almost all of my friends I've known for years!"

Growing up, we're often encouraged to "buck up" and blink back our tears. People especially encourage boys to be strong and not cry. What's the most common response to the sight of a child crying? "Don't cry!" For many if not most people, this leads to associations of embarrassment and even shame with crying, especially if the crying occurs in public or in front of anyone other than a cherished, loved significant other.

However, though we're all told early and often not to cry, as it turns out, sincerely powerful emotions—especially those powerful enough to cause tears—are quite influential in connecting with other people. If you can get yourself to experience a level of vulnerability with someone to the point where you're moved to tears, you will be able to relate to that person—and he or she can relate to you—on a much deeper level.

This doesn't mean you should walk around the office crying all the time, of course. What it does mean is that you should create a safe atmosphere with the people around you at work and at home and get to a place of trust and vulnerability with them so that if tears do come, you can embrace them and celebrate the fact that the tears will bring you closer together.

Though two of the executives I cried with that day are no longer with our company, years later I still feel as connected with them as I do with nearly anyone else on the planet. I'll be there for them when they need me, and I'm sure they'll be there for me if I need them.

As it turns out, crying, in fact, is for winners.

FAST First **A**ction **S**teps to **T**ake:

1. Write down an inventory of your ability to get in touch with your emotions and cry. When were the last five times you cried, and what were the circumstances of each incident?
2. Find a partner (or two) to experiment with, ideally someone you're not too close with already but whom you trust and who trusts you. Create an opportunity to be vulnerable with each other in a safe place. Think about what it would take for you to feel comfortable crying in this space and in front of this person and then try to replicate those conditions elsewhere.
3. As you continue to encounter people, don't be afraid to be vulnerable, and if the urge to shed tears overtakes you, don't fight it or blink it away. That sincere vulnerability connects you to others in a powerful way.

20. The Platinum Rule Always Trumps the Golden Rule

"Dave, why in the hell did you do that? Just because you thought you were helping the situation doesn't mean you were. In fact, you ruined everything!"

I could envision the irate man on the other end of the phone, steam coming out of his ears as he yelled at me. The crazy thing is that I really did think I was helping the situation. As it turns out, though, what I'd actually done was piss off a major business partner.

We had been business partners for over a year, and it was that company's responsibility to drive sales for our firm. But lately its sales force hadn't been delivering results. I was frustrated and disappointed, and I wanted to help. In essence, I had my own sales force start offering the product this man's team had been selling. I truly thought he would be thrilled to have more support selling the product. After all, I reasoned, if one of my partners added more manpower to a joint venture, I would be very happy. If it would make me happy, I figured, it surely would make him happy as well.

The Golden Rule, right? Wrong. He wasn't happy. In fact, he was furious: angry that I didn't tell him about my plans in advance, upset that he might be wasting his own resources, and generally disappointed in me and the partnership.

When I thought about it from his perspective, I realized how I might not have been helping but instead might have been seen as meddling or distrusting or just wrong. He had a job to do, and I was interfering with it in his eyes. I didn't agree with that perspective, of course. Then I realized something even more important: It didn't matter whether I agreed with it; his perspective was what counted, not mine.

We all grow up learning about the simplicity and power of the Golden Rule: Do unto others as you would want done to you. It's a splendid concept except for one thing: Everyone is different, and the truth is that in many cases what you'd want done to you is different from what your partner, employee, customer, investor, wife, or child would want done to him or her.

With that in mind, I came up with the Platinum Rule: Do unto others as *they* would want done to *them*.

The Platinum Rule is decidedly more difficult than the Golden Rule. It's easy to know what you want, but it's much harder to put yourself in another person's shoes, walk around in them, and understand that person's perspective.

But although it's harder to do that, it's much more powerful in business and in life. The Golden Rule, as great as it is, has limitations, since all people and all situations are different. When you follow the Platinum Rule, however, you can be sure you're actually doing what the other person wants done and assure yourself of a better outcome.

In the business classic *How to Win Friends and Influence People*, Dale Carnegie shares the following parable, which I think gets at the heart of what I talk about when I talk about the Platinum Rule:

> Personally I am very fond of strawberries and cream, but I have found that for some strange reason, fish prefer worms. So when I went fishing, I didn't think about what I wanted. I thought about what they wanted. I didn't bait the hook with strawberries and cream. Rather, I dangled a worm or grasshopper in front of the fish and said: "Wouldn't you like to have that?"

Why not use the same common sense when you are fishing for people?

Do unto others as they would want done to them.

If I had dangled a worm or a grasshopper in the business relationship I described, I certainly would have talked to our business partner about my proposed plan and avoided an unfortunate outcome. But I didn't. I failed to realize the important adage: Platinum trumps gold.

If you're doing a great job listening, mirroring, and validating, and if you're being your authentic, vulnerable present self, you should be able to see the other person's perspective and apply the Platinum Rule without a problem. But even if you're having trouble figuring out exactly what the other person wants, the beautiful thing is that if you're in doubt, you can just ask. We all know the adage about what happens when you ASS-ume something, so rather than assuming, simply ask by saying something such as "If I were you, I'd really want X to happen. What do you want to happen?"

Their reply will give you your answer. And then you, too, can go platinum.

FAST First Action Steps to Take:

1. Write down a description of a conflict you've had with another person. The entire description should be from the other person's point of view. Get inside that person's head and imagine walking in his shoes to accomplish this.
2. When faced with your next decision involving another person, ask yourself, What would she want done? Use the answer to inform your decision.
3. Practice the Platinum Rule. When in doubt about the other person's perspective, simply ask that person.

5

Influencing People

21. Help People Come Up with Your Idea

"I don't like your idea," my client said dismissively from across the table. "It's too risky. Legal would never approve it. It'll never fly. Sorry."

Those words, uttered at me from across a basement mall management office, cut like a knife, because I *knew* I had a great idea for this client, the owner of a shopping mall in Queens, New York. It was in the middle of the recession in 2008, and our idea was to "stimulate the economy" by giving out cash to random people on the streets of New York City with a call to action to come to the mall to win even more cash.

Of course, the idea was that once they got to the mall, whether they won more money or not, they'd shop, and I was confident that giving cash away on the streets of New York would create quite the buzz. Heck, it might even win some awards for being such a clever marketing stunt. But none of that would matter if our client didn't like the idea enough to green-light it. I felt dejected. Defeated. Demoralized.

Luckily, the next day, I accidentally discovered a key principle in the art of people when I was summoned again into my client's basement office.

"I have a great idea, Dave," the client said. "What if we gave out stickers along with the cash? The stickers would have an explicit call to action to visit the mall and also have the address for a website where people could visit to see all of the official rules and regulations. What do you think?"

"I think you have a great idea," I replied. "So can we make it happen?"

"Well, now that we agree on my idea," the client responded optimistically, "I think we can get it all approved by legal and upper management. I'll get back to you quickly on this promotion. I'm really excited about it."

This client had gone from superpessimistic about my idea to superexcited in less than twenty-four hours. Why? Because somehow in those twenty-four hours she had come to see the whole idea as hers. I simply let her believe that, and the rest was history.

How can you apply this principle to influence others? Though I stumbled upon it in this situation, you can increase the likelihood that someone else will take credit for your idea easily:

1. Never say, "I have an idea" (or "I have a great idea" or any kind of idea) despite my lucky success in this case. Take the pronoun out of the equation.
2. Instead, paint a picture of the broad brushstrokes of your idea or the results of that idea. Let the person you're trying to influence color within the lines and visualize the rest herself.
3. Alternatively, paint a picture of the converse of your idea. What are the negative implications of not embracing it? In this situation, the other person will envision the downside of not adopting your idea and then come up with a solution to prevent it from happening.
4. When the other person says anything close to your idea, fully embrace it and enthusiastically praise her for *her* idea.
5. If what she's proposing is not quite what you want, subtly suggest additions or deletions to her idea, reminding her along the way that she has *such a* great idea and this might make it even better.

Let's examine how this could work in two real-life situations. First, imagine you want an associate at work to help you take on a project. If *you* suggest that he take on the project, he may not jump at the chance excitedly. Instead, you can say, "That project is going to have quite the spotlight on it. I bet our CEO is going to handsomely reward whoever delivers it." Then sit back and enjoy it when your associate comes up with the idea to help you with it. Alternatively, if you'd prefer to go the negative route, you can say, "I hope I can get this project done by myself. If I can't, I think the CEO is going to be mighty disappointed and blame our whole team."

"I have an idea," your associate will then say. "I can help with the project!"

Perhaps at home you want your husband to do the dishes but don't want to nag him. "I've been thinking," you might say. "What if we decided to get all paper plates and cups and utensils? It would be a lot more expensive, but we wouldn't have to do so many dishes anymore." If instead you wanted to go positive, you might say, "After all our chores are done, let's snuggle up and order a movie."

Pretty soon, either way, you might hear from your husband, "I have an idea. Let me go do the dishes."

I'm sure you'd be okay with that even if it wasn't your idea.

By the way, we did execute that promotion for the mall. It generated over a million dollars' worth of earned media for our client and earned our agency its first award, all because of one idea. The question is: Whose idea was it?

FAST First **A**ction **S**teps to **T**ake:

1. Write down an idea you have for something that involves another decision maker. Ideally this should be something you haven't asked for yet or often.
2. Write down the vision you can paint (both positive and negative options) to help the other person come up with your idea.

22. Passion Is Nothing Without Persistence

"Dave from Radio Disney! Are you ever going to stop calling me and singing to me?" asked the voice on the other end of the phone, but in a playful, upbeat way.

I was in shock that Brenda Fuentes actually had picked up the phone. Our history quickly flashed back in my head before I knew how to respond.

Brenda Fuentes was a regional marketing manager for Burger King at the time, and I was a local sales rep for Radio Disney Boston. I had been assigned the Burger King account as a target, and my goal had been to get hold of Brenda, gain an understanding of Burger King's marketing needs in the Boston area, and ultimately try to sell her radio advertising and promotion.

But getting hold of Brenda Fuentes had proved difficult, to say the least. She worked from home, and the first three times I had called, I had gotten her voicemail. I didn't have her email address and this was the early days of the Internet (2001), and so the only way I could reach her was by phone.

I was determined to get hold of Brenda. Even if she was going to say no to my sales pitch, I wanted to know I had given it my all. I knew how many other salespeople must have been calling her and leaving her voicemails: other radio salespeople, local TV sales reps, print ad reps, and early Internet advertising reps, to name just a few categories of salespeople. With all this competition, how would I ever get her to take my call? Then I thought about the one thing I had that none of those other reps had, and that was Radio Disney.

For me Radio Disney wasn't just a job; I loved the station and its bubble-gum pop music. It was both fun to listen to and safe for the whole family, including little kids. I decided to get creative in my persistence. I would continue to call Brenda, but I would leave only one voicemail per week. Each time I left a voicemail message, however, I would sing a parody of a Radio Disney hit song into the phone. Eventually, I figured, this creative strategy of leaving her messages to the tunes of popular songs would get her attention and help me stand out from the countless other phone calls and voicemails I assumed she got.

For instance, one week I sang to the tune of an N-SYNC hit, "Call me back, please, won't you give us a try? Bye Bye Bye." The next week I left a message to the tune of a popular Britney Spears song, saying, "Oops, I got your voicemail again. Please call me back soon; I can't wait to talk then." I called every day and left voicemails every week for seven full weeks, and she never did call me back. Then, finally, in week 8, on call number 37, Brenda Fuentes finally picked up the phone, giving me a chance to sell her.

As it turns out, one of the biggest differentiators between those who successfully influence others and those who don't is *persistence*. Many people talk about passion, and of course passion for one's idea, product, or belief is important, but many people have passion. Far more people have passion than have persistence. This is true for salespeople, for entrepreneurs, and for anyone chasing anything or anyone else whom many are pursuing. When it comes to the art of people, persistence is what makes the difference.

Persistence is defined as "firm or obstinate continuance in a course of action in spite of difficulty or opposition." In other words, when the going gets tough, you keep trying.

But persistence isn't trying things twice or three times or even four times. Persistence is trying until you get what you want or go down swinging. Persistence is continuing until you are certain beyond a shadow of a doubt that it's time to move on and collect the lessons from the failure. Persistence is trying until you drop. Persistence is thirty-seven phone calls.

Persistence isn't trying things **twice** or **three** times or even **four** times. **Persistence** is trying until you **get what you want** or **go down swinging**. **Persistence** is **trying until you drop**.

I had refused to give up on Brenda Fuentes and Burger King. Sure, along the way there were days when I felt dejected and demoralized. I was made fun of by colleagues for my silly songs. There were moments when not only did I begin to doubt that passion and persistence would get me results, I began to worry that all they were getting me was a lot of wasted time and embarrassment.

And then, on call number 37, Brenda Fuentes answered the phone. But this wasn't your average opening sales call. After all, she already knew me pretty well from all those voicemails. Now at last it was my opportunity to get to know her better by asking good questions, listening, validating, and letting her come up with my great ideas to help Burger King market itself.

Forty-five minutes later, we had a follow-up plan for me to present a proposal for Radio Disney advertising and promotions around twelve upcoming Burger King grand openings. One week later, I had signed an agreement for over $50,000 in revenue, which would generate over $10,000 in commissions for me. Even more interesting is that fourteen years later, I still have a great working relationship with Brenda Fuentes.

All from seven singing voicemails and thirty-seven phone calls. If I had called only thirty-six times, it probably never would have happened. But I persisted until there were thirty-seven, and everything changed.

FAST First Action Steps to Take:

1. Write down something that you really want from someone but that won't be easy to get. (Who would you like to meet more than anyone? What client would you like to land? What business idol would you like to have lunch with?)
2. Use your passion and creativity to come up with a plan to pursue this person doggedly in an inventive, original way.
3. Put your plan into action and be persistent. Make as many attempts as it takes to make this vision a reality.

23. Don't Sell It, Storytell It

My whole family of twenty-one people was sitting down to eat Thanksgiving dinner. It was one of the most stressful moments of my life, but the stress wasn't coming from getting together with my extended family.

You see, I had been bidding for the URL storytellit.com, and the auction was literally about to expire: The auction's end date and time was Thanksgiving Day at 4:30 P.M. My company had developed an app to help small businesses tell stories across the social Web, and I had spent the previous month trying to secure a domain name on the Web for it.

This project was harder than it sounds. We originally had called the app Storyteller, but when I called the owners of Storyteller.com, they told me the name wasn't for sale even though it wasn't being used. Thinking, "Everything's for sale at one price or another," I asked the owner, "What if I hypothetically offered $100 million for the domain name?"

"Not for sale," he replied, and hung up on me. Thus, I had to conclude that our app would not be called Storyteller.

Next, I went to the owners of Storytell.com, a lovely older couple who told us we could buy their domain for $100,000. That was a huge bargain compared with $100 million, but for a start-up it was a price that was too high to pay.

We next turned to storytellit.com, where it turned out there was an auction taking place for the domain name. Excited, I put in a bid of $12, only to be immediately bettered at $17. I didn't want to start a bidding war, so I resolved to bide my time and then put in my best bid and try to win the domain right at the end of the auction.

The only problem was that the end of the auction was literally the same time as the start of my Thanksgiving dinner. I couldn't leave something this important to anyone else, and so at 4:15 P.M. on Thanksgiving Day 2013, I sat in front of a computer while ten feet away my family members began to sit down to a mouthwatering feast.

I thought we had the winning bid at a mere $22 until one minute before the end of the auction, when someone swooped in and bid $27. That bid also apparently extended the auction for five minutes. "No problem," I thought. I proceeded to bid against this other person while my turkey proceeded to get cold.

Bids of $32, $50, $100, and $150 immediately followed, and I was beginning to wonder whether we'd ever have a domain name for our new app. Meanwhile, my family was beginning to wonder if I'd ever join them at the dinner table. It was a tense situation, to say the least, as each time a higher bid was made, it extended the auction another five minutes.

Then, magically, my bid went unanswered. For $165 we became the proud owners of storytellit.com. But the lesson here isn't about how to win an auction. It's about why I wanted that URL so badly in the first place. The lesson is about the power of stories.

Nobody likes to be sold to, but everybody likes a good story. Storytelling persuades, storytelling compels, and storytelling conveys emotion to people in a way that nothing else can.

Storytelling is a much better communication tool than selling.

Storytelling actually sells products, services, and ideas better than selling can.

Luckily, in today's online world, you don't have to be a Hollywood producer or a published author or have a podium to sell a story. You can be a salesperson sharing an ebook on LinkedIn. You can be a blogger sharing your story on Tumblr or Medium. You can be a dentist sharing a photo of a smiling patient on Facebook. You can be a jewelry store owner sharing a picture of an engagement ring that a customer just bought on Twitter.

Everyone can use social media to tell stories.

Moreover, social media allows you to tell stories at scale, potentially reaching exponentially more people than ever before. But even if you're one-on-one with someone or in front of four to six people in a boardroom, telling stories captivates people in a way that no other kind of talking does.

Whether it's online or offline, storytelling influences others. By the way, that story about storytellit worked, too: I told it on my blog as part of the launch plan for the product storytellit. The article generated 50,000 views and thousands of downloads and performed far better than any ad would have in selling our product.

FAST First **A**ction **S**teps to **T**ake:

1. Write down something you want to sell someone. If you are not a salesperson, think of an idea you want to get someone to adopt (e.g., getting your child to make her bed).
2. Think of a personal story that's relevant to the idea you want to convey. Write down the story: beginning, middle, and end, characters, emotions, and all the rest.
3. Practice telling the story to another person (*not* selling).
4. When you're ready, try sharing the story with the person you want to sell and/or writing the story publicly on a blog.

24. The Paradox of Persuasion: Shut Up

"Dave, look, I like your passion and excitement for Dunkin' Donuts, and it sounds like you have a lot of really interesting, exciting things to offer with Radio Disney," said Shannon, a longtime marketing lead for the Dunkin' Donuts brand who was based in Massachusetts. "But I can barely get a word in here. How can you learn about our specific marketing needs if you do all the talking in this conversation?"

I was so embarrassed when I heard this. I had worked really hard as a persistent salesperson for Disney by incessantly calling both Shannon and her gatekeeper assistant, Betty, to get this face-to-face opportunity, and now I was blowing it by talking too much.

That was a mistake I made often early in my sales career, and it's one I still occasionally make as an entrepreneur and CEO. There is no question that many of the best salespeople and the best leaders are filled with passion, positivity, ideas, and enthusiasm. Those qualities serve us well in many cases. Our passion and enthusiasm are contagious, for instance, and as a result many people want to be around us.

But these strengths sometimes come with a nasty side effect. Often, precisely because we get so passionate and excited about an idea, an opportunity, or a product, we can't seem to stop running our mouths about it. The result is that once the people who wanted to be around us so badly are actually around us, they pretty quickly start wishing we'd just shut up and listen. As Dale Carnegie wisely explained:

> If you want to know how to make people shun you and laugh at you behind your back and even despise you, here is the recipe: Never listen to anyone for long. Talk incessantly about yourself. If you have an idea while the other person is talking, don't

wait for him or her to finish: bust right in and interrupt in the middle of a sentence.

The point is that to influence others, you have to know when to shut up and listen.

It may sound like the ultimate paradox that listening to others is the key to influencing them, but for those who are not yet convinced, here is a recap of all the reasons listening is so much more powerful than talking:

1. Listening allows you to understand the person you want to influence so that you can tap into his unique goals, dreams, needs, and wants.
2. Listening gives the other person an opportunity to feel heard, which often leads to feeling appreciated and respected and even liked or loved. It is much easier to influence someone who's feeling this way.
3. Listening gives you an opportunity to think. We can listen three times faster than we can talk, and so listening gives us extra time to think, prepare, and reframe what we want on the basis of what we're hearing.
4. Listening, along with mirroring and validation, helps lonely people feel connected and great. This is even more contagious and powerful than feeling great around a positive, high-energy talker.
5. Listening increases the chances that the other person will talk about her pain or her organization's pain, that is, the problem that you can try to solve.

No matter what you have to say, offer, sell, or convince someone of, it is always more effective to demonstrate genuine, authentic interest in the other person by listening and asking questions and then listening some more than it is to talk at that person. Of course, eventually you have to talk to share your idea or product or otherwise make your case, but if you've laid the groundwork by listening, that part is actually surprisingly easy.

Recently, I was selling our latest company's software product, Likeable Local, over the phone to Mike, the brother of a dentist who happened to be a retired police officer. The software was made for small businesses, especially dentists, which at the time was the only vertical on which we were focused.

I had an online demo of the software ready to show and had booked thirty minutes with the officer, who I had been told helped do the marketing for his brother's dental practice. After a brief introduction to let him know who I was and how the product had come about, I began asking questions. I was genuinely interested in how a retired police officer could end up doing the marketing for a dental practice, and so I asked questions about it, got more curious, and asked more questions, all the while sitting back and *listening instead of selling.*

Twenty-five minutes in, I heard the following from Mike: "You know what, I'm running out of time, but this has been great. Let's get started with this software. I can't wait to really dig in and see what it's all about. Just let me know how billing works."

I hadn't even had to demo the product, and the deal was done.

It sounds crazy to say that all you have to do is shut up and listen and you'll be able to influence people to do what you want. But just as I persuaded Mike to purchase my software without even showing him what he'd be buying, thousands of decisions to buy are made every day by people who don't realize how they've been influenced to make that decision. Often they've been influenced by the people around them, who are simply listening quietly and asking good questions.

Thankfully, that day with Shannon, I reacted quickly and positively to the embarrassment of being called out. I recovered, asked questions, shut up and listened, and soon afterward enjoyed closing the largest contract I had ever sold at that time.

FAST First **A**ction **S**teps to **T**ake:

1. Write down something you want to sell someone. If you are not a salesperson, think of an idea you want to get someone to adopt (e.g., getting your child to clean her room).
2. Plan to spend thirty minutes with the person you want to sell, focusing solely on listening, asking questions, and getting that person to talk about her pain and problems.
3. Set up the time and spend it listening to the other person (*not* selling).
4. Note the results. How can you become a better listener?

25. Walk into Every Room Like You Own It

"Okay, Dave, here's your ticket. Just look straight at the security guard, make eye contact, give a nod, and walk straight in."

Those were the tips given to me by Gary N, my short-time business manager, just seconds before I walked into the 2003 American Music Awards in Los Angeles, California. I could not have been more excited. I recently had fashioned myself a D-list celebrity after starring on the reality show *Paradise Hotel* on Fox, but this was an A-list event. After seeing my show, Gary had reached out to me to help me get a hosting gig and had said he was very well connected in the entertainment industry. Not knowing any better and lured by the prospect of getting famous, I had told Gary he could represent me, and now he was taking me to one of the biggest events in Hollywood.

In we walked, and a few seconds later I heard Gary say, "Paula! How are you?" He was talking to Paula Abdul, who was right beside Randy Jackson, both of *American Idol* at that time. I was a little starstruck but mostly remained composed when he introduced me.

"So great to meet you guys. Big fan of the show, though I can promise you that's one reality show you'll never find me on as a contestant," I joked, having fun.

"Come with me," said Gary, and the next thing I knew we were in a celebrity gifting area. I had heard of this practice but didn't know the details: Essentially, celebrities went from station to station getting free stuff from vendors who wanted them to talk about their products. I walked around and filled a bag with all kinds of great stuff: headphones, cologne, and jewelry, to name a few items. It was incredible!

Then, as I was walking out of the gifting station, I saw her: Standing before me was the most beautiful creature I had ever laid eyes on. It was the actress Jessica Alba, and at that point I finally lost control.

"You . . . you . . . you . . ." I stammered. "You're so beautiful."

"Thank you," she said, and promptly walked away.

"Wow," I thought. "That was simultaneously both amazing and humiliating."

"Come on, Dave, let's go find some empty seats," said Gary. "The show's going to start soon."

I was confused. Find some seats? Weren't we assigned seats on our tickets?

Little did I know at the time that the ticket I had been handed by Gary wasn't a valid ticket to the American Music Awards at all. I looked down at the ticket only to see "Crew" stamped on it—and "2002." Since it was 2003 and we weren't crew, I was pretty concerned.

"Don't worry," Gary said. "We're already in; that was the hard part. Now we just need to find empty seats. Shouldn't be a problem. Everyone gets so drunk at this event, they're barely in their seats at all."

I hadn't yet gotten over my shock at seeing Jessica Alba, and now I was even more shocked. How could we get in if the tickets were bogus?

"I told you to make eye contact and nod. I didn't want you to worry; I wanted you to be confident. You were, and now we're here. Now let's go get some seats."

As we made our way toward "our" seats (we ended up in the nineteenth row for the first half of the show and the sixth row for the rest), I didn't know whether to be furious or exhilarated. But I knew there was a lesson to be learned from this experience:

Walk with confidence.

My wife and I call it WWC for short. What WWC means is that you walk into a room as if you belong. Make eye contact. Nod your head. Say hello with enthusiasm. When you look the part and act the part, suddenly you are the part.

Some people call this "fake it till you make it," but I don't like the idea of inauthenticity. I like the idea of confidence (not cockiness or arrogance, of course, but quiet confidence with your posture, your eyes, and your walk).

Now, obviously I'm not advocating trying to walk with confidence into the American Music Awards, the White House, or the Super Bowl. Heck, if I'd known I didn't have a valid ticket, there's no way I would have been able to walk right in like that. But you can use this strategy to own a room. WWC into every event you go to and every meeting you walk into and you'll be more likely to walk out a winner. Walking with confidence will help you influence gatekeepers whether they're security guards at award shows or receptionists at offices. Tell yourself you don't belong and you won't. Tell yourself you totally belong and you will.

I had a few embarrassing seconds with Jessica Alba that night, but that's a moment I'll never forget. And I owe it all to Gary N and a little WWC.

FAST First **A**ction **S**teps to **T**ake:

1. Write down an environment, event, or location at which you typically feel nervous or out of place.
2. Make a plan to WWC into the room the next time you visit that location. Include your clothes, accessories, posture, and anything else you'll need to increase your confidence.
3. Walk with confidence into the location. Be sure to make eye contact, hold your head up, and own the room like the rock star you know you are.

26. You Never Get What You Don't Ask For

"So, Dave," said the frustrated young woman who had been working harder than anyone else on the sales floor and thought she'd been doing everything right. "Why am I not seeing more success in sales?"

Nicole was a good salesperson for our software company, Likeable Local. Good but not great. What made the difference between good and great for her was one very simple thing, the same thing that often makes the difference between successful people and very successful people. It took listening to her on a product demo for me to find that out.

I sat in on a demo Nicole had with John, the owner of a jewelry store in Boca Raton, Florida. He was an older gentleman, uncomfortable in general with social media, and Nicole did an excellent job of building rapport early, listening, mirroring, and validating his concerns. He was wary of doing social media on his own but was not sure how much time or money he had for software like ours. Then Nicole began showing John our product via the Web and did a great job of explaining the key features that answered his concerns.

Everything was going quite well until the end of the call.

"Okay," said Nicole. "So do you have any questions for me?"

"Nope," John said. "I'll think about it and call you back later."

"Okay, sounds good," Nicole said. "I'll call you back tomorrow if I don't hear from you. Bye."

She hung up the phone and looked up at me, exasperated at not having made the sale but perhaps clued in to what I was going to say.

"Almost a perfect job, Nicole!" I cheered. "So what did go wrong there?"

"I don't know," she replied. "Everything was going so well right up until the end. I guess I'm just struggling with closing sales."

"Let me ask you something," I said. "Did you actually ask him for his business?"

"I guess not," Nicole said. "I mean, I listened and then told him everything I thought he needed to know to make a decision."

"But did you actually ask him to make a decision, Nicole?" I was getting frustrated at this point but was confident we were getting somewhere.

"Well, I guess I didn't," she said.

It may seem obvious, but many people make this mistake.

They don't actually ask for what they want.

And guess what? You probably won't get what you want unless you ask for it.

Sure, you still have to do all the legwork in advance. And sure, you're not always going to get a "yes" when you ask. But you're much more likely to get a "yes" if you actually ask for it than if you wait for it to materialize out of nowhere.

And no matter what, if you don't ask for it, you're not going to get it.

Many people are so afraid to get a "no" that they don't ask for a "yes." The ironic thing here is that they're virtually guaranteeing getting a "no" by not asking for a "yes."

Embrace the fear of "no." Then ask for the "yes."

Nicole was doing an excellent job as a salesperson, but with one major flaw: She wasn't asking for the "yes." Once she got some training from her manager, Nicole quickly became one of the top salespeople in the company, doubling her earnings within six months. It turned out that getting the "yes" was simple. She just had to ask for it.

No ask is too crazy.

Embrace the fear of "**no**." Then ask for the "**yes**."

Here's another example of how simply asking for something—even something that seems totally crazy and audacious—can get you the "yes" you want. In 2005, shortly after Carrie and I got engaged, we had a problem. I really wanted to have a large wedding, the kind where I could invite everyone I knew to share in our joyous celebration. But Carrie and I didn't have enough money to host a traditional New York wedding and invite everyone we knew.

Luckily for me, Carrie, a marketer by trade and temperament, had a brilliant out-of-the-box idea: We would partner with a minor league baseball team to create a wedding-themed promotion, sell sponsorships, and get a ballpark wedding paid for—a wedding that we could invite thousands of people to attend. Sponsors could get great value in the promotion, which probably would generate buzz and media attention, and we could get a huge wedding at virtually no cost to us. As a die-hard baseball fan, I thought the idea was perfect, but of course it would require persuading willing partners to sign on to make it work.

We pitched the Brooklyn Cyclones, a minor league affiliate of the New York Mets, whose general manager, Steve Cohen, fortunately liked the idea enough to give it a shot. Next, we successfully pitched 1-800-Flowers.com to sponsor our flowers, Smirnoff to sponsor our alcohol, Entenmann's to sponsor our desserts, After Hours to sponsor our tuxedos, and several other local and national sponsors, totaling about $100,000 in trade value. That wasn't all; by also asking sponsors to donate cash to the David Wright Foundation, we were able to raise $20,000 for the National Multiple Sclerosis Society through our wedding.

To most people, asking companies such as 1-800-Flowers.com and Entenmann's to sponsor a wedding would seem preposterous if it occurred to them at all. After all, these are major corporations that sponsor big-ticket events such as the World Series and the Super Bowl. Why would they be interested in such small potatoes? Yet they were, and although I still can't be completely certain why they said yes, there is one thing I am sure of: We never would have gotten them to sponsor our dream wedding if we hadn't asked, because you don't get what you don't ask for.

That is how on July 8, 2006, I got married to the love of my life in front of five hundred friends and family members (and five thousand strangers) on a baseball field where instead of walking down the aisle we walked underneath the bats held up by the Cyclones. It was an amazing wedding with an amazing partner.

As it turned out, the wedding was also an amazing marketing and public relations promotion for our vendors and sponsors. It generated about $20 million in earned media through coverage on CBS's *The Early Show,* ABC's *World News Tonight,* CNBC's *On the Money,* the *New York Times,* and hundreds of blogs. Our vendors were so thrilled with their return on investment, in fact, that a couple of them asked us what we could do for them next. We couldn't get married again, so we started our first company instead.

You never get what you don't ask for.

FAST First **A**ction **S**teps to **T**ake:

1. Write down three things you want from people right now but haven't been asking for. They can include things as small as a sale from a new customer or as large as a raise from your boss or more attention from your husband.
2. Let go of any fears, embarrassment, or shame you have about asking for things.
3. Set yourself up with opportunities, in person or via a phone or video call, to ask these three things of people. You can do this. Remember, a "no" is better than not asking for what you want.
4. Dream up something big that you want from someone, even if you think he'll never say yes to the idea. Ask for it. What's the worst that could happen?

6

Changing People's Minds

27. It's Better to Be Happy Than Right

"Why do you always need to be right?" she growled.

My wife, Carrie, was not in a good mood. We had been arguing about childcare, and I was being very stubborn about a baby-sitter I wanted to let go because recently she had been texting constantly on the job, including while she was driving our kids around town. I wanted to fire her immediately, and Carrie wanted to give her a chance to correct the behavior before considering that.

I had been relentless in my argument. "Carrie, it's not safe for our children," I had said. "Carrie, we need to do right by them," I had said. "Carrie, she's not going to be able to change," I had said. And though my voice had remained calm, I hadn't given an inch on what I wanted.

"Dave, let me ask you something," my wife said. "Is it better to be happy or right?"

"Trick question," I snarled back. "It's better to be both happy *and* right!"

At first I was proud of my clever retort. Then I thought about the situation a bit more. As strongly as I felt about my position, I wasn't going to change my wife's mind then and there. It just wasn't going to happen. This baby-sitter had been with us for over three years and had become very close with us, truly part of our extended family. Although I believe in hiring slow and firing fast, the reality is that it takes time for most people to come to a decision and execute it.

I had to make a decision right then and there: be happy or be right. It's hard for me to accept not winning any argument, but I chose the former.

"Okay, I understand how you feel," I said. "She's become part of our family, and it's very hard to make a decision to let her go." I was mirroring Carrie's argument back at her (we talked about this in Chapter 15). "You must feel so conflicted," I said, validating her (see Chapter 16).

"You know how I feel, so I don't need to repeat that," I continued. "I'll just say I support you in every way possible, and I'm going to choose to be happy right now." I smiled, nodded, hugged my wife, and calmly walked away.

It was difficult, because I'm not always perfect at following my own advice when it comes to communicating with my wife. But I pulled it off that time: I walked away, and instead of continuing to try to change Carrie's mind, I made sure she felt supported even if I disagreed with her. I chose being happy over being right.

Then, the very next afternoon, a funny thing happened. Carrie had been working from home that day while the sitter was there with our kids after school. Apparently, the sitter continued to text incessantly with the children (and my wife!) right in front of her. I received a phone call from my wife minutes later.

"Dave, we've got to let the sitter go," she said. "I've seen the texting with my own two eyes now. It's too much. Let's make the move now." I didn't argue, and we discharged the sitter the next day.

Did I change Carrie's mind? Maybe. But it's more likely that she came to the conclusion that I was right on her own. Did I change my own mindset about the situation? Absolutely. The thing is, it's nearly impossible to change someone's mind. Dale Carnegie put it this way, and I agree: "A man convinced against his will is of the same opinion still." I'd even go so far as to say that arguing usually just helps the other person solidify his opposition to you. In contrast, it's much easier to state your case and then change *your own mindset*—to choose happiness—and let the other party sit with the situation until she comes around to your position on her own.

To win influence, don't change the other person's mind. Just change your own mindset.

Remind me of this the next time I get into an argument with my wife, won't you?

FAST **F**irst **A**ction **S**teps to **T**ake:

1. Write down an account of the last time you got into an argument with someone. Did you choose being right or being happy?
2. Prepare to choose happiness the next time you get into an argument with that person. This definitely takes a lot of mental preparation. Be sure to do the mental legwork ahead of time so that you're ready in the heat of the moment.
3. When the next argument happens, calmly state your case and then say you are choosing to be happy over being right, smile, and politely walk away. You might be surprised to find that you get what you want after all.

28. Always Manage Up

It was 9:05 A.M. when I walked into the Radio Disney office on a cold February day in 2002. I knew I was supposed to be in at nine on the dot, as my new manager, Sam, had recently made explicitly clear. But I still struggled with mornings, and I had had a late night, and there had been traffic on the way into Boston from the northern suburb of Somerville, from which I was commuting. Anyway, forget excuses: Why should it matter if the top salesperson at the company is a few minutes late as long as he can perform?

It mattered to my boss, apparently. As I hustled past his office to my desk, I glanced to my left and saw him at his desk, staring at his watch and shaking his head. I knew I was in trouble.

Moments later, as I was settling in at my desk, there was a knock at my door. "Can I have a minute with you in private, please?" my boss asked.

"When you're late, it's a sign of disrespect," Sam said. "It doesn't matter whether you're thirty minutes late or three minutes late. I've told you this before: Being on time is very important to me. It's disrespectful to your colleagues when you're late. It's disrespectful to me."

That was when it hit me. My manager's obsession with my punctuality wasn't about me; it was about *him*. He was a relatively new sales manager and wanted to see the whole sales team respect him, especially his punky young hotshot sales guy. When he saw his top salesperson showing up late, even by just a few minutes, I'm sure he was concerned that the whole team would lose respect for him. Even if this wasn't conscious or intentional, it was an important dynamic. As soon as it clicked, I knew what I had to do: make it less about me and more about him.

"I hear you," I said, and then mirrored and validated him. "You must feel awfully disrespected by my showing up late."

He was nodding, and I could tell I was making progress. "How can I show you more respect?" I asked.

"Well, for one thing, you can be on time!" Sam snapped back. So much for progress.

"I get it," I replied. "Don't be late. I will work on that," I said, and he went on his way.

But I knew that not only did I need to work on my lateness, I needed to work on making him feel more respected by me. I needed to manage up.

The next three weeks, I worked hard to get to work and sales meetings on time. But more important, I worked hard to make sure I was showing respect to Sam and showing others how much I respected him. I listened to him without interruption, told him when I thought he had good ideas, and showed him that I was taking his directions and advice seriously. I managed up.

Then, three weeks later, I asked Sam for a few minutes of his time.

"Sam, I know punctuality is very important to you, right?"

"Yes, Dave. And I have noticed that since the last time I spoke to you, you've been very punctual. Thank you for that," he said.

"My pleasure, Sam," I said. "I have a lot of respect for you. I've been thinking. Is it the punctuality that's more important or the hours put in in a day?"

"Both are important," Sam replied. "You set an example for the whole sales team, and when you're late, it sets a bad example for the whole team. You understand that, right?"

"I do," I replied. "I totally understand. Say, I've been thinking—I'm just not a morning person, Sam. But I have a lot of respect for you and want to do right by you. I'm happy to work late every night, so instead of staying until five, I can stay until six or six-thirty." I paused.

"Hey, I have an idea," Sam replied. "What if you started at nine-thirty and worked until six instead of nine to five-thirty? That way you'd never be late!"

"Great idea, Sam," I answered enthusiastically. "You're the best!"

From that point, I showed up at the office at nine-fifteen, nine twenty-five, nine-thirty—sometimes I even showed up at nine forty-five—and it still didn't matter. Incredibly, I had gotten Sam to make a complete reversal in his attitude about what time I showed up at the office. How did that happen?

I took the focus off me and put it on him. I also met his needs (in this case, respect), I managed up, and I let *him* come up with the idea to solve the problem (see Chapter 21). Those four things combined to create a solution that got my manager off my back about being late and kept both of us happy and productive.

When can you use this technique? It comes in particularly handy whenever someone has a problem with you or something you're doing, especially if it's your boss. The key idea is take the focus off you and whatever you're supposedly doing wrong, figure out what the other person really wants or needs, give that to him, and eventually let him make the correct decision (that is, give you what you want).

Note that managing up doesn't mean kissing butt or being a yes man. It means having a very solid understanding of what's important to your boss and the leaders at your organization and then paying attention to delivering on what's specifically important to them. Think of managing up as the "Platinum Rule" for organizations: Think like your manager and you will reap the benefits of getting your way when you need it most.

I went on to work productively in sales for Sam for another year after that incident. We didn't always see eye to eye on things, but he always respected me, and he never again looked down at his watch—even the day I showed up to the office at ten-fifteen.

FAST First Action Steps to Take:

1. Write down the name of the person at work you need to manage up to. If you're the CEO, it might be a partner, an investor, or even a client.
2. Write down the five things that are most important to that person. (If you don't know these things, ask around.)
3. Make sure that in your day-to-day work you are focused on doing the things most important to your manager. Pay special attention to making sure that both your manager and your peers see you doing those things well.
4. Then go back to your manager and ask for the one thing—whether it's a raise, a promotion, or permission to come in a little late in the morning—that you most want.

29. Go Beyond the Humblebrag

"So excited!!! We won the WOMMIE award for word-of-mouth marketing excellence for the second year in a row!"

That Facebook update from me, unfortunately, was followed quickly by a private message that read: "Enough already, Dave! I know you won an award or two, I know you're excited about it all, but stop shoving all this self-promotion in our faces!"

This Facebook message in the fall of 2009 from a casual friend stung, probably because there was some truth to it. Our company had just won its second consecutive word-of-mouth marketing award for a campaign I was really proud of, and so I had been sharing the news proudly and liberally on Facebook, Twitter, and LinkedIn. I guess this person was connected to me on all three networks, had heard the news at least three times, and was sick of hearing from me about the award.

Still, I was upset and confused about the situation. On the one hand, I was genuinely proud of our work and wanted to share the good news. Plus, I've always believed in the art of self-promotion, and social media seemed like a great way to put the word out and get attention. On the other hand, I certainly didn't want to get attention for being an egomaniacal braggart.

I took the feedback to heart and tried to develop a more modest attitude toward posting to social media. In other words, when I had good news to share, I still shared it, but I tried to be humble, grateful, and not overly self-promotional in my social media updates. Meanwhile, unknown to me, the word *humblebrag* was being added to the Urban Dictionary. I'd never heard that term, but as it turned out, it described exactly what I'd begun doing. For example, when we won the same award for the third consecutive year, I shared it, but this time my social media updates looked like this:

"So honored and humbled to have received the WOMMIE Award for the 3rd year in a row! Thanks to the whole team @Likeable Media!"

On the surface, this seemed a lot better than the more traditional social media brag. I was proud but grateful and appreciative at the same time. The problem with sharing accomplishments on social media (aka bragging), however, is there's no tone or body language to help convey your meaning, and that means it's very easy for people to lose the context and not get your intention right. As a result, it's next to impossible to establish a voice that won't turn some people off when you share, especially if you are sharing information that could, in the absence of context, be interpreted as bragging.

Thus, I wasn't that surprised when just three minutes after sharing the news about our third consecutive award, I received a private message from a different friend on Facebook: "Dude, what's with the humblebrag? Just gloat, man, no need to fake being humble when you are dominating the award circuit!"

I felt exasperated, as if I couldn't win for losing, and I couldn't believe that humblebrag was even a thing. It seemed as though no matter what I did, I couldn't share my joy about accomplishments without offending some people. Did this mean no more sharing such accomplishments? For some, the answer to that question might be yes. For me, it was no, with two key caveats:

1. Be unafraid but as authentic (noncontrived) as possible in sharing accomplishments on social media.
2. Heap lots of authentic praise on others via social media as well.

The first point is simple: You're going to be judged by people no matter what, so just be your authentic self and stand behind that authenticity no matter what people may say.

The second point is important, too: Be quick to praise others in social media (and face-to-face). Authentic praise and compliments make people feel good, help them feel more comfortable in sharing their accomplishments, and, most important, show the world that you're not all about yourself and are just as apt to sing another person's praises as your own.

The art of self-promotion has always been both important and challenging, and social media has made it even more so. It was over eighty years ago that Dale Carnegie wrote that the secret of success is to "speak ill of no man . . . and speak all the good I know of everybody," and those words couldn't be truer today. After all, open up your Facebook, Twitter, or LinkedIn app on any particular day and you'll see one noisy update after another, with marketers and self-promoters dominating news feeds. It can be tough to cut through all that chatter, let alone do it in a way that feels modest and not too bragging or egotistical. But it can be done by following the two simple steps discussed above.

The challenge for you, then, is to scroll through your social media news feeds looking for opportunities to praise, congratulate, and promote others: your friends, colleagues, and followers. Be generous in retweeting people. Promote the heck out of everyone.

Two great things happen when you do this. First, when you authentically have something of your own to promote, you'll be much less likely to be judged as a braggart—or, worse, a humblebraggart—by others. Second, you'll have a line of people excited to promote you and return the favors from all those times you promoted them.

The musician Taylor Swift is my favorite example of someone who promotes herself and her accomplishments authentically while continuing to support and promote others, including her many fans. Here are a couple of her tweets that do just that:

Taylor Swift
@taylorswift13

Thank you, Baton Rouge!!! You were amazing.
And you looked like THIS:

11:00 PM - 22 May 2015

So @russwest44 just made my night......
https://instagram.com/p/3ABgtwiiMI/
10:41 PM - 22 May 2015

"hahah it really does sound like Starbucks Lovers..." -my mom just now who is SUPPOSED TO BE ON MY SIDE

Smh.
10:41 PM - 22 May 2015

You may not be as famous as Taylor Swift, but you certainly can be as authentic and as generous as she is. And, like her, you can get beyond what others might call bragging or humblebragging and share your own success publicly while changing people's perception of you for the better.

Tune in to my Twitter feed today and you'll see me unabashedly sharing my latest work or achievement, but you'll also see me promote just about anyone who asks. Don't believe me? Just tweet me (@DaveKerpen) with a link to your latest work or accomplishment with the hashtag #artofpeople, and I'll gladly retweet you to all my followers.

FAST First **A**ction **S**teps to **T**ake:

1. Take a look at your last twenty social media updates and do a quick audit. How much are you promoting yourself versus promoting others? Ideally, you want to strike a balance of no more than 30 percent promoting yourself and at least 70 percent promoting others.
2. Make a plan to increase both your own authentic self-promotion *and* your promotion of others in your life.
3. Audit your next twenty social media updates and compare them with the previous twenty. Have you helped people see you as someone willing to praise others and unafraid to share his or her own accomplishments?

30. Make Time Your Friend

"I wish you had more time for me."

Have you ever heard this from someone important to you at home or at work? I have countless times. As it turns out, time is our most precious asset, and although everyone wants your time, you need to protect it fiercely if you are to be successful. For the most part, people always want more of your time than you are able to give.

As a social media entrepreneur and author, I get contacted each week by dozens of people who want my help or want to work with me. In a way this is by design: I put myself out there, and since responsiveness is so important to winning friends and influencing people on social media—as well as being one of my personal core values—I reply to each and every person who asks for my help. Before I got as crazy busy as I am today, I used to meet with anyone and everyone who reached out to me.

Even if you're not as active in social media as I am, if you're a leader, you're probably often solicited by salespeople, asked for help by random colleagues, and presented with many requests—or demands—for your time on a daily basis. If you're at all like me, you try to be nice—or helpful—and take every call, reply to every email, or even agree to every meeting.

I had a powerful experience a year and a half ago that changed all that. I had attended a conference hosted by the Entrepreneurs' Organization's founder, Verne Harnish, on strategic business planning. Verne is a brilliant mentor and trusted friend, and something he said that day really stuck with me: "You can understand your professional strategy with one quick look at your weekly calendar."

Naturally, I immediately took a look at my weekly calendar on my phone and saw that it was filled up with meetings and phone calls with people I didn't know who probably would make no difference to my business or my life. Sure, I might be able to help them, but my first priority is my family and my second is my employees, investors, and customers. Why was I sacrificing time with them to take all those meetings with strangers? Not only did the meetings and calls take me away from my focus and from time spent on the things that mattered; thinking about them before and afterward continually distracted me.

After that, I decided to start a program I call "office hours." Each week, for two hours on Thursdays, I now meet with people who have reached out to ask for help, fitting them into fifteen-minute time slots.

This includes students, former employees, wannabe entrepreneurs, and salespeople. It even includes readers (you can sign up at http://ScheduleDave.com). I still reply to and try to help each and every person who comes my way. But once the time slots are full, they are full, and people have to sign up for the following week's office hours, or the next week's hours, and so on.

This has made it a lot easier for me to say no to meeting requests or at least say, "Not until my next office hours opening three months from now." As it turns out, this method not only helps me protect my time but also functions as a terrific filtering system. The people who genuinely want help end up meeting with me when my schedule allows, and the others tend to go away.

You don't have to create an office hours system and meet with everyone who wants your time, of course. But you do need to figure out a way to prioritize your time, the most precious asset you've got, carefully. Whether it's saying no to people who are less important to you or limiting the time you agree to give them, the reality is that you can prioritize only a limited number of relationships in your life at work and at home. Are you totally happy with the way you're prioritizing your time today?

With my office hours system, some people may have to wait

awhile to chat with me, but if they are willing to wait, they'll eventually get their shot during those two hours a week. More important, my calendar is now more reflective of my priorities, as 95 percent of my workweek is spent on what matters to my employees, investors, and customers.

Most important, I've been able to change my system so that I also have time for the people in my personal life who are the most important to me: my wife, family, and friends. I even have a little open time on my calendar to think and write.

Since my quick creation of office hours and a scheduling system, people have stopped saying "I wish you had more time for me." Instead, I've started hearing "Thanks for prioritizing me."

FAST First **A**ction **S**teps to **T**ake:

1. Take a look at your weekly online or offline calendar for the last three weeks (seven days, four hours a day). When you analyze the time you spent with each person and doing each activity, are you happy with how you're prioritizing your time?
2. Develop a system—feel free to borrow my office hours system or create one of your own—to limit or curb the less important tasks and conversations in your life and increase the time you spend on the more important ones. Check in with the people you want to spend more time with and let them know what you're doing.
3. One month from now, review how well your new system is going. Check in with the people you wanted to spend more time with and ask them what they think. Recheck your calendar and note any differences in the way you're prioritizing your time with people.

7

Teaching People

31. Be a Model

"You've got this, Mr. Kerpen," said Mrs. Mary Ann Wilson, my supervising teacher, to me just before I began my very first math lesson as a student teacher in her first-grade classroom. "Just remember to model it, then model it again, and then let the kids try on their own."

"Oh, and one more thing, Mr. Kerpen. I'm going to go run a couple of errands. Don't worry; I'll still be in the building. Be back in twenty minutes. Break a leg!"

With that, she walked out of the room, leaving me completely alone with twenty-two six-year-olds to whom I was about to teach my first lesson. I was caught off guard and definitely was scared. But I was also determined to do what Mrs. Wilson and I had practiced: modeling.

I gathered the children in the meeting area and began a mini lesson in subtraction. I showed them an example they could relate to (starting with ten cookies and then eating two) and walked through exactly how I solved it. Then I did another problem (ten cookies and eat four) and then another one (ten minus seven).

"That's a lot of cookies to eat in one sitting!" said Mariah, but she and the rest of the kids were getting it, and I was excited about that. I finished the lesson by sending the children to their seats with ten Oreo cookies for each table to do some subtraction problems with and then eat. By the time Mrs. Wilson got back to the classroom, just about all the students in the class could do basic one-digit subtraction problems as long as they had cookies in hand.

"Looks like you did a nice job, Mr. Kerpen," she said. "Now finish the lesson by modeling one more problem."

Even though most of us don't work as schoolteachers, we all have to take on the role of a teacher every day in one way or another. No matter who your students are, there is an enormous difference between *telling* them how to do something and *showing* them how to do it. Thus, when you have something to teach, whether it's a subtraction lesson to six-year-olds or a task to a colleague at work, the very best way is to do it yourself, showing your students every step along the way. It's also important to remember that you know how to do it and the other person doesn't. This seems obvious, but too many people try to teach others something and quickly get frustrated when the students don't get it right away. As we've talked about in other sections of this book, the best thing to do is to put yourself in your student's shoes. If *you* weren't getting something at first, wouldn't you want to be shown how to do it again (and again) without judgment?

Patience is the key here. The best teachers are often the most patient ones. By modeling each step along the way and simplifying every part of a task, you can teach just about anything to just about anyone. Just imagine that your student is a first-grader.

I never taught first grade again, but I did teach middle school math for three years nearly a decade later, and I've had the fortune of getting to teach lots of people a whole lot of things over the course of my career no matter what work I was doing. Each time, I remember the importance of modeling as I learned it from Mrs. Wilson, my model teacher.

FAST **F**irst **A**ction **S**teps to **T**ake:

1. Write down a list of several things you'd like to teach the people in your life, with at least one thing being from work and one being from home.

2. Choose one of the things you'd like to teach and write down the steps in as simple, clear, and concise a way as possible. Think of this as writing a lesson plan.
3. Put your lesson plan into action and teach this task to someone, making sure to model each step along the way yourself. Remember to be patient.

32. Soar with Your Strengths—and Theirs

"What's wrong with him? What's wrong with me?" I asked my wife rhetorically.

I was absolutely exasperated about the situation. One of the earliest employees at our first company, Chris, was really struggling. He was the nicest guy: smart, dedicated, and loyal. He was a great observer of people and had a strong if soft-spoken presence.

But as an early employee of a small, fast-growing company, Chris had to wear a lot of hats. The latest one that we needed him to wear was that of office manager, and Chris was struggling to pick up the required skills.

It couldn't have been his fault, though, I reasoned, because he was too talented and passionate. It had to be mine. I just wasn't teaching him well enough.

I went to my wife and business partner, Carrie, then the chief operating officer, to ask for help. It was really my first time in a role in which I was managing people, and she had managed a radio sales team successfully before, so I knew she could help.

"Hmm," said Carrie. "I think I have a book for you."

She went into her office and pulled a book from her shelf: *Soar with Your Strengths.* The big idea in the book, she told me, was to understand your strengths and then use them to teach others. Furthermore, the idea was to help others identify *their* strengths and teach and manage to those strengths as well. Rather than looking at Chris's weaknesses and trying to teach around or fix them, she said, I could better understand his natural strengths and teach him to be even better at those things.

I liked those concepts a lot, and so I read the book and then began to put the principles to work. First, I quickly realized that office managing (and operational work in general) was not a natural strength of mine. If we needed Chris to learn to be a better office manager, I wasn't the best person to do the teaching. That was okay; I had to soar with my strengths.

Then, more important, we realized that in teaching Chris how to be a better office manager, we weren't soaring with Chris's strengths, either. Chris simply wasn't a desk-and-paperwork kind of person; he liked to be out and about among people. Chris was always a great reader of people and a fine judge of character. We didn't want to waste his skills, and so I ended up teaching him how to do something that tapped into these strengths: recruiting. He soon became our first human resources manager and recruiter, going to college fairs and job fairs and helping secure the best talent we could find.

The office manager work? We found someone else to do it: Maria, who was detail-oriented and a much better fit. More important, I didn't train Maria. Carrie, a better person for the job, did that.

Everything changed as soon as we changed our point of view about what to teach and who would do the teaching. It's about soaring with strengths.

How often do you have to teach something to a reluctant student? How often are you a reluctant teacher because you don't feel completely confident and competent in what you are supposed to teach? It won't help anyone if you're not the right teacher or your student isn't the right person for the skills or tasks. Sure, there are times when all people must learn something they are reluctant to learn. But there are also times when you can find someone more appropriate to do the teaching or learning and allow your original student and yourself to better soar with their strengths.

Remember, you can't fit a square peg in a round hole. All people can learn and be successful at something as long as they soar with their strengths.

You can't **fit** a **square peg** in a **round hole**. All people can **learn** and **be successful** at something as long as they **soar** with their **strengths**.

By the way, after two solid years of recruiting for us, Chris realized that his passion and proclivity for being out and about and observing others, and his desire to be away from an office job, were so strong that he ended up leaving the company for another field entirely. He's been a happy and successful police officer ever since.

FAST First **A**ction **S**teps to **T**ake:

1. Write down a list of several things you've been trying to teach others that aren't your greatest strengths. Determine whether anyone else at work or at home could take on the teaching of these skills or tasks.
2. Examine one colleague or friend and think about one thing you would like to teach that person. Write down her strengths and how you will teach in the context of those strengths.
3. Put your plan into action and teach this one thing to the person by playing into her strengths. How can you take an area your colleague or friend is already good at and make her even better?

33. Don't Be a Teacher (or a Manager); Be a Coach (and a Student)

"She's not a teacher; she's a monster!"

That was what I said to my friend Kev about our eighth-grade social studies teacher, Ms. Macusor. She had just thrown me out of the class for talking after I had been three minutes late and was asking Kev what I had missed. I ended up having to go to the principal's office even though I really hadn't done anything wrong.

This was just one day of the many in which I struggled with Ms. Macusor. It wasn't like I was a bad student; I got good grades in all my other eighth-grade classes. But Ms. Macusor was, well, consistently mean, and not just to me. She yelled at the class a lot. She often didn't allow students into her classroom if they were even thirty seconds late. Instead of helping kids who were struggling, she was very critical of students who "didn't do their work right." My friends and I felt that she was always trying to get us. I'm sure she had a good reason for the way she acted, but it didn't change the results.

Many of us have had at least one experience with a teacher like Ms. Macusor. If you haven't, you may have had an experience with a manager or leader like her, someone who is seemingly always angry or upset at something, tries to tell you what to do but offers little help or support, and is generally a negative person.

Ms. Macusor didn't inspire, lead, or even teach very much. The only thing she inspired was fear. She's an extreme example, of course, but too many people who are teachers or managers have elements of Ms. Macusor in their personality, attitude, and behavior.

Contrast her with Doc Rubenstein, my tenth-grade chemistry teacher, who taught me one of the most important lessons I've ever learned about leadership.

"It's not my job to teach you. It's your job to learn. I'm just here to coach you along the way," Doc would say to us on a typical day. He was one part teacher, one part coach, and one part cheerleader—always positive, helpful, and encouraging.

Each day, Doc would greet us with a smile and get us started on a chemistry lesson or experiment. We did most of the learning on our own or in small groups, and he would go around the room to see how each of us was doing. He told a lot of jokes, had a lot of one-on-one conversations, and had a lot of fun with us. He probably did less formal teaching than any teacher I've ever had, yet he was one of the best.

A close second, though, might have been Mr. Boyle, my twelfth-grade psychology teacher. Mr. Boyle would always tell us, "I'm a student, just like you. I've just been learning this stuff a little bit longer than you've been."

I thought that was quite profound, and it stuck with me. Mr. Boyle didn't think he was better than us. He didn't try to pull rank on us. He didn't tell us what to do. He considered himself one of us—a student on the path to learning and betterment—and his actions matched that attitude. Mr. Boyle was another one of my favorite teachers, even if he preferred the label of student.

In the workplace, many of us end up in manager or teacher roles without sufficient training. However unintentionally, it's easy to end up like Ms. Macusor when one is put in a situation like this: trying to control, micromanaging, and being overly critical. Of course, not only did we hate Ms. Macusor, we didn't learn from her. It's important to avoid adopting a managerial style like Ms. Macusor's, not only because you don't want your teams and employees to hate you but because it won't work!

Instead of embracing the manager or teacher title, embrace the title of coach. Good coaches are cheerleaders while still teaching. Coaches are there to help us win, to help us succeed, and to be supportive. These are the traits that not only will make everyone happier but will help you teach and manage better, as well.

Bad coaches, by the way, do lead through fear. There are sports coaches who yell at their players and are every bit as intimidating as Ms. Macusor was. But the good coaches don't do that. They're more like Doc: supportive but holding their players accountable. Good coaches embrace teaching when necessary but also embrace hand-holding when necessary. Good coaches are there with the players from start to finish, and the players succeed as a result.

If you can layer in an element of Mr. Boyle's style and be part student, that's even better. The truth is (and the best coaches and managers understand this), no matter how much you know, no matter how much experience you have, and no matter what position of authority you're in, you, too, have a lot to learn. If you embrace this idea, your humility will shine through and your students (or direct reports) will respond.

Fear-based management and teaching can work temporarily. People may be scared of the consequences of not listening to you, and so they may pay attention, listen to you, and even perform for you. But study after study shows that this is just temporary. Over time, when you lead with fear and micromanagement, when you make yourself as a teacher instead of your students the center of attention, the results get weaker. It's also so much less fun!

Embrace the adventure of learning with your students or direct reports and coaching them along the way to mutual success. Everyone wins, and nobody goes to the principal's office.

By the way, the last I heard, Ms. Macusor had left teaching and become a cashier at a department store in New York. Here's hoping she's not mean to her customers.

FAST First **A**ction **S**teps to **T**ake:

1. If you're a manager, make a list of the people who report directly to you. If you are not, consider which people you influence as a teacher (kids, friends, colleagues) and write down at least three names.
2. Write down the names of three of your favorite and best schoolteachers from your youth. How did their ability to coach you and/or their willingness to learn from you affect your performance and your choice to listen to them?
3. Reflect on and write down how you can become a better manager and/or teacher at work or at home by better embracing your role as coach or student the way your favorite teachers did.

34. Don't Hold Yourself Accountable

"Why do we keep missing our goals?" Ben asked my eight-person entrepreneurs group. "Because we've been missing one key ingredient. That all changes, right now."

For the previous year, our group, which meets monthly, had been working on goal achievement. Eight driven, successful entrepreneurs were determined to grow as individuals, and the goals activity was bound to help. At the beginning of the year, we had each set metrics-driven personal and professional goals that we could come back to and report on to the group. At each monthly meeting, among other things, we all reviewed our progress on our goals.

There was only one problem: We weren't making any progress. Each month we were honestly reporting on how well we'd done that month, and each month we were coming up short.

I began to wonder if perhaps we had set goals that were too difficult to achieve. My goal, for instance, was to exercise at least thirty minutes a day at least four times a week, and I just wasn't hitting it on a consistent basis. I was trying to lose weight, and I knew that consistent exercise (or lack thereof) was an important part of the equation.

"Bullshit," said Ben. "We're not hitting our goals because we're not accountable enough. Starting today, we'll each have a goal accountability partner. You are to check in with your partner at least once a week. First up, reassess all goals together and make sure they're SMART goals (*s*imple, *m*easureable, *a*ttainable, *r*ealistic, and *t*ime-bound). Then, instead of you updating the group at our monthly meeting with your progress, your partner will update the group on how well you're doing and you will update the group on how well your partner is doing."

Ben was a man on a mission, and although there was definitely some pushback and hesitation among the group, we collectively decided to embrace the new plan. Andy would be my personal accountability partner, and I would be his. The meeting ended, and the new era of goals work began.

A funny thing happened over the next several months. We all went from missing our goals to hitting them! Encouraged by this success, I began to get very competitive, and not just for myself but also for my accountability partner, Andy. I wanted him to be able to report that I'd hit my goals each month, and so I worked harder than I had before to hit them. At the same time, I was thrilled to report that Andy was hitting his goal of performing and tracking random acts of kindness. The rest of the group was doing great, too.

The only thing that had changed from one year to the next was that we all had and were accountability partners for one another. And we had gone from failing miserably to achieving success!

There are a million business books claiming that we should all hold ourselves accountable for our actions and our performance both at work and outside it. But in reality, we should be letting *others hold us accountable* for our successes and failures. Why? Because when you're accountable to another human being you trust and respect, it makes you *want* to work harder to achieve the goals you set. Plus, it helps you stop rationalizing and making weak excuses. For example, even if "I can't go to the gym this morning because it's raining" sounds perfectly reasonable in your head, the simple act of saying it out loud to another person helps you see how lame an excuse it actually is. However, when you're accountable to too many people, it's like being accountable to no one. Thus, the best scenario is to find one accountability partner who can help you and whom you can help.

Whether you are a manager or not, teaching people about the

power of goals and accountability partners, finding accountability partners for them, and helping facilitate the coaching and reporting process will have an enormous dual effect. First, you'll find that your people will become more accomplished and confident. Second, and more important, *you* will become more accomplished and confident as well.

The three keys to making this work are as follows:

1. Assigning accountability partners who trust and respect each other
2. Setting SMART goals together
3. Checking in at least once a week, ideally twice a week, with one another

If you can teach this process to yourself and others, you will find that everyone will get more things done faster.

In the year that followed Ben's proclamation, I ended up developing much better exercise habits, and thanks to that and to eating well, I lost nearly fifty pounds. I owed the credit to my partner and to the process of accountability we set. Since then, I've implemented the system with nearly a hundred employees. Of course, not everyone is successful all the time. But my people report much better success with their goals, with an accountability partner standing proudly by their side.

FAST First Action Steps to Take:

1. If you're a manager, use a list of the people who report directly to you to create a set of accountability partners. Include yourself. If you are not a manager, think about who you'd like to be an accountability partner of yours and approach that person.

2. Ask each of the accountability partners to set one SMART goal together. It's always best to start with just one goal. Decide how often you will check in on each other and report progress.
3. Carry out the process for at least three months and compare the success you and your people experience with accountability partners with what you achieved in the past. You'll never go back to holding only yourself accountable again.

8

Leading People

35. There's No *I* in *Team*, but There Is an *I* in *Leadership*

"Are you kidding me, Dave? There may be no *I* in *team*, but there sure as hell is an *I* in *leadership*. Now quit farting around and step up and become a leader!"

I had just been admonished by a mentor of mine, and it hurt. Robb High was a senior consultant who had worked miracles for thousands of agencies and brands since leading his own agency to great success many years earlier. We had been having a conversation fairly early on in my first business, which happened to be an agency, and I had been telling him about how I believed in everyone being equal, working together as a team, and supporting one another.

"That's all fine, Dave," he had said. "I'm all for teamwork. But every team needs a leader."

Robb was right. In an effort to have everyone feel that his or her voice was heard and that everyone was important, I had failed to become an effective leader. Robb had a blunt, direct, and powerful way of saying things, and I understood what he meant right away. But the problem was that I had no specific idea how to become a leader.

Very few people take leadership classes in school, yet so many are called on to become leaders. Chances are, you have chosen to become or have been asked to be a leader at some point in your life. But what does leadership mean? Does it mean leading by example? Yes. Does it mean inspiring others? Absolutely. Does it mean doing the right thing (after figuring out what the right thing is)? Yes. Leadership includes all these things. In fact, leadership can mean many different things to many different people, and that is both a good thing and a bad thing.

Very **few** people take **leadership classes** in school, yet **so many** are called on to **become leaders.**

I didn't have a succinct definition of leadership until I met Verne Harnish, who in time would become a great mentor, friend, and investor for me. Verne is the founder of the Entrepreneurs' Organization (EO), a global network of ten thousand CEOs, as well as a longtime leader, CEO, and author. I joined EO soon after Robb had admonished me to become a stronger leader. Then I read Verne's excellent book *Mastering the Rockefeller Habits*, and soon thereafter I met Verne.

He told me there were three and only three things on which great leaders have to focus:

1. Setting and communicating the overall vision for your team
2. Making sure you have the right people in the right seats on the team
3. Making sure you have enough resources and money to help the team succeed

"If you do those three things well, everything else will fall into place," Verne told me.

The interesting thing is that this framework can work whether you're a leader of one person, ten people, a hundred people, or a thousand people. No matter the size, scope, or mission of your team, and whether you're a CEO of a small business or a manager of a team of two people in a Fortune 500 organization, if you can get these three things right, you can be an excellent leader. My wife and I have even applied this methodology to leading our family of five.

Here's how you can apply this simple framework within your team or organization. First, set and communicate the vision. This is most important but often is overlooked. What is your grand mission? Your purpose? Your overall vision for how things will be? It's important to develop this, because everything else can fall into place once you have it. If you don't have a clear vision for your team or project, it's worth taking the time to develop one now. It's never too late to get the train on track! Once the vision and mission are established, it is essential to overcommunicate it! Talk about it with your team, email it, share it as much as possible. Some companies literally put it up on their office walls.

The next job of a great leader is to make sure to have the right people in the right seats. This is true whether you're the CEO of a Fortune 500 company or the CEO of your home, and it starts with you. Are you the right person to accomplish the vision in light of the current size and scope of the team? Ideally, you are, but if you're not, a great leader will recognize this and find someone more appropriate to lead. For instance, often a great entrepreneur/founder isn't the best person to run his or her own company after it has achieved a certain scale, and ends up stepping aside in favor of a more seasoned CEO.

Beyond you, it's essential to make sure you have the most talented, most appropriate people surrounding and leading the way beside you and that they, too, are in the right seats. There are really only two questions to consider in making this determination about your people: How capable are they of doing their jobs? and How aligned are they with your vision and values? These two questions are critical in finding the best person for any essential position, whether at work or in your personal life.

When we recently hired a nanny and household manager for our family, we interviewed over twenty people before choosing one. Some were very qualified for the job, but we weren't convinced about their alignment with our values. Others shared our vision and values, but we weren't convinced of their capabilities. Ultimately, we found and chose a rock star, Joyce, to join our family. Joyce has a great attitude, great skills with babies, and a terrific résumé and came with impeccable recommendations. I consider the decision to choose Joyce to work with our three children in our home one of the most important leadership decisions I've ever made, period.

The final thing a leader must do is make sure she has enough resources and money to help the team succeed. Whether this means applying for more funding, getting creative, or somehow figuring it out MacGyver-style, it's your job to make sure the team has everything it needs to succeed so that the team members don't need to worry about it. In other words, you worry about getting all the money and resources so that they can focus on doing their jobs and making the magic happen.

I once had a senior executive at Likeable Local who was excellent at his job but was always nervous about our cash flow. We were an early-stage start-up that was not profitable yet and were raising money from investors to stay afloat and grow. I was taking care of making sure we had enough money in the bank, but he was still nervous about us running out of money, and it affected his ability to do his job. I'm not sure whether it was his fault or mine—probably a little of both—but the situation didn't work, and we had to part ways. That experience solidified how important I believe it is for leaders to make sure there is always enough money in the bank. It's simply essential to make sure your team doesn't have to worry at all so that instead of focusing on pinching pennies, the team members can focus on what you hired them for.

I'm so thankful to Verne Harnish, who taught me these three things to always remember as a leader, and to Robb High, who taught me about the *I* in *leadership*. Thanks to both of these mentors and many others, I've been able to become a better leader.

FAST First **A**ction **S**teps to **T**ake:

1. Write down what makes you a leader, or, to put it another way, write down who looks to you for direction and guidance. (Remember, regardless of the size and scope of your organization, you can consider yourself a leader.)

2. Audit how well you are doing in setting and communicating vision. Ask people in the group you just defined if they know what your grand mission is. If you don't have a mission, it's time to come up with one. Then work on communicating that vision clearly and consistently.
3. Ask yourself if everyone in the group you lead is in the right seat. Are there people with talents that are being underutilized? Is there someone who has been promoted above her level of competency and expertise? If you find instances like this, shift people's job descriptions and responsibilities to better reflect what they are best suited to bring to the team.

36. Mirror Neurons, and How a Good Mood Goes a Long Way

I was having a real bummer of a day. I had received word that morning that a major investor who I thought was going to give us $500,000 had pulled out. Worse, I got news that my dad, who was living in a nursing home, had lost his teeth. Finally, I looked at our sales numbers and saw that we were way down on the month against our forecast.

I was about to lead our weekly team meeting, but luckily, I had an interview for our Likeable podcast first. The interview was with John Bates, a fellow author and speaker and an expert on public speaking. He started the interview by asking me if I had ever had a bad audience as a public speaker. I replied, "Sure, I've had some horrible audiences. They were nonresponsive, didn't laugh at my jokes, didn't interact on Twitter the way I wanted, and overall they sucked."

"I've got good news and bad news," John said. "The bad news is, it's probably you that sucked, not them. The good news is, for all the great audiences you've had, and I'm sure you've had some good audiences, it was probably because you were on that day and didn't suck."

"Whoa," I thought while continuing this live interview. "I can't believe he just totally blamed me for my bad audiences."

John went on: "The reason I say this is it's backed by real science. You see, we all have mirror neurons that 'mirror' the emotions of the person who's speaking to us. A mirror neuron is a neuron that fires both when an animal acts and when the animal observes the same action performed by another animal. Thus, the neuron 'mirrors' the behavior of the other, as though the observer were itself acting. So if you're a public speaker and you take the stage in a bad mood, your audience will likely sense it and become a 'bad' audience. If, on the other hand, you take the stage in a great mood, your audience's mirror neurons will sense that, too, and they will become a great audience."

"Wow," I said, and wrapped up the interview. Intuitively, it made sense to me. I knew that when I was in a bad mood, people could sense it, and when I was in a great mood, people could sense that, too. But I had never heard of the science of mirror neurons before, and so I hadn't realized how powerful this phenomenon is. While John Bates was giving his explanation of mirror neurons to address the power of mood and intention in public speaking, I realized that this lesson was equally applicable to leadership.

Every time I speak at my company, our employees are listening, and their mirror neurons are in action. When I am in a bad mood, I'm sure the team members can sense it and potentially end up in a bad mood themselves, and there's no way they'll perform as well as I want them to while they're in a bad mood. I realized that no matter what mood I was in, it was my job—no, my obligation—to brush it off and get myself to a positive, inspirational place no matter what.

That's obviously easier said than done in many circumstances. We all have good days and bad. Heck, we all have good *moments* and bad in every day that goes by. But if we want to persuade or inspire the people we're speaking to, we need to check that at the door. Whether you're a public speaker in front of a thousand people, a CEO in front of ten managers, or a manager in front of one team member, you have a choice each and every time. You can choose to stay in a bad mood and risk having that mood rub off on your followers, or you can get yourself to a positive place and transfer that positive energy.

How? In Chapter 35, I talked about the importance of setting and communicating a vision. Well, I believe the best way to get to a superpositive place quickly when speaking to another person or a roomful of people is to (re)focus on that vision and then communicate it. People love to hear about where they're going, and they love a strong, bold vision—no matter what. Of course, you need to have a strong, bold vision to do this, but once you do, you can get positive and share that vision no matter what.

That day had begun as a really terrible, horrible, no-good, very bad day. But thankfully, it took a more positive turn—just when I needed it most—after my interview with John Bates and his lesson about mirror neurons. I was determined to put my learning into action immediately at our companywide weekly meeting later that day.

I went to the bathroom, looked in the mirror, thought about our vision, and got myself psyched up for the team meeting. Once I felt sufficiently positive, I went back out, began the team meeting, and in front of forty employees said: "Imagine five years from now. All of us are at the NASDAQ, about to ring the opening bell in honor of our IPO. We've got a hundred thousand happy small-business customers at the time, and our hard work has finally paid off. You won't need to imagine this, because if we all work hard and focus on the mission, we will all get there together."

I might have had a terrible day leading up to that meeting, but thanks to my lesson from John, I ended the day and that team meeting strong. Nobody in our company knew how bad my day had been, and people walked away feeling excited and inspired and determined.

I'm not saying you should lie—I'm as much for transparency as anyone—but your job as a leader is to get the most out of your followers, and sometimes that means sweeping your bad mood under the rug. Now that you know about mirror neurons, you know how powerful an influencer your mood is. Each and every time you speak to your team, consider how you can keep a superpositive attitude and focus on the vision and the big picture.

FAST First **A**ction **S**teps to **T**ake:

1. Write down an experience in which you were in a bad mood and addressed your team. What was that like? How about an experience in which you were in a terrific mood and addressed your team? What was that like?
2. Make a plan for the next time you're having a bad day and need to talk to your team (or anyone, for that matter). How can you quickly snap out of it and focus on the big picture or vision?
3. The next time you are in a bad mood and need to speak, put your plan into action and get those mirror neurons working with you, not against you.

37. How to Get Everyone to Want to Be Around You, with One Word (Maybe Two)

I was annoyed at having to take the day off from teaching to attend a United Federation of Teachers conference, and so far the conference, to be honest, had been quite a bore. It was 2004, and I was both a teacher and a union chapter leader and was spending the day away from school to get some professional development. So far I had been majorly disappointed, but that was about to change with a session that would change my life forever. I sat down in the front row in an effort to stay attentive and got ready for the session to begin.

A tall, good-looking older man took the stage.

"How are you doing today?" he asked the audience.

I figured it was a rhetorical question, but I found myself nonetheless answering quietly in my seat, "Fine."

"Most of you are thinking 'Fine,'" he conjectured. "Some of you might be thinking 'Good' or 'Great' or 'Lousy.' These days, some of you might be thinking of the word *Busy*, too."

I was amazed at how he knew what I'd been thinking, and from the nods around me in the crowd, I think everyone else was, too.

He continued: "I'm going to let you in on a secret. I'm going to tell you the word I always use when people ask me how I'm doing. It's an extremely powerful word, and it begins with the letter *F*."

"This is getting good, finally!" I thought. I waited with eager anticipation for him to reveal the *F* word.

"Someone ask me how I'm doing," he insisted. I immediately called out from the front row, "How are you doing!?" to which he replied: *"Fantastic!"*

"Fantastic," he said. This was the word he always used when people asked him how he was doing and the word that he recommended that others use. He claimed that by using this word, you'll attract whoever you're talking to and make that person want to be around you, because no matter how anyone else is feeling, fantastic is probably better, and who wouldn't want to feel fantastic? Plus, he argued, by saying "I'm fantastic!" with a big smile, you can actually put yourself in a better mood, which is contagious as well.

He went on to talk about other principles of leadership and influence, but frankly, I don't remember much else of what he said. What I do remember eleven years later is his contagious positive energy and the word *fantastic*.

Soon thereafter, I put his concept to the test with staggering results. As it turns out, most times people ask "How are you?" they're expecting either the word *fine* or a similarly lukewarm response. When people hear "I'm fantastic!" instead, heads turn. Over the seven years or so that I've put this simple principle into action, I've come to the undeniable conclusion that this is a powerful statement that makes you irresistible to others. Some of my favorite replies to "I'm fantastic!" include the following:

1. "Oh, my God, what are you on?"
2. "I'll have what you're having."
3. "Sign me up!"

It's amazing how one simple word can draw people in and get them pumped to be around you. In the years that have followed, I've added one more word to this repertoire that I have found to be equally powerful. This is a word that I got from the effervescent, superpositive consultant Sam Horn: *Imagine*.

Imagine is a powerful word because it gets people dreaming and thinking about what could be. Everyone loves to imagine at least a little bit, so when we give people permission to imagine by using the word, they appreciate it. Try it and you'll see how excited people get at the very thought of using their imaginations.

When people hear **“I’m fantastic!”** heads turn.

I've put these two words, *fantastic* and *imagine,* into my regular vocabulary, and I've been blessed and amazed by how responsive people have been through the years. Of course, you need to be authentic in your use of those words; I wouldn't advocate telling people you are doing fantastic on the day your dog dies. But really, even if you're not feeling great, you can always take a step back, remind yourself to be grateful for how good you've got it relative to so many others, and realize that life is pretty fantastic after all. Imagine that.

FAST First **A**ction **S**teps to **T**ake:

1. Write down five things that are fantastic about your life and five things you can imagine for your team and/or family.
2. The next time someone asks you how you're doing, consider answering, "I'm fantastic!" Note how the other person responds when you say that.
3. The next time you address your team, consider using the word *imagine* to paint a picture of what might be. Note your team's reaction to that word.

38. Always Be the One to Give the Bad News

I've got a problem," I told Verne Harnish, a business mentor of mine, in September 2009. "I believe in always staying positive, but looking at our numbers, we have some real challenges."

I was getting ready for our quarterly managers' meeting for Likeable Media and just didn't feel right about putting a positive spin on things. We had missed our numbers and almost definitely would have to lay some people off. I knew that I had to stay positive, but I didn't want to avoid reality. "What can I do?" I asked Verne.

I had to share "the brutal facts, the brutal truth," he said. Paraphrasing the great business author Jim Collins, he continued, "As important as it is for you to remain positive, it's even more important for you to make sure that you and your team address the brutal facts and reality of your situation at all times. Only then can you fix it."

That made sense to me, but I was still nervous. My senior executives were used to seeing me as a superpositive, vision-focused leader, and I didn't want to be a bummer at our quarterly retreat. But I trusted Verne—and Jim Collins—and so I knew I had to be transparent. I took a deep breath and began to plan my opening remarks for the meeting.

The next day, I began with the brutal facts: "Look, team, the reality is, we've missed our numbers and we are going to have to make layoffs. This isn't going to be pretty, or good, or fun. But if we all address the realities head-on, we can get through this together, and imagine how strong we'll be when we come out of it all."

As promised, the next two days weren't easy, but an interesting thing happened. My executive team appreciated how transparent I had been with them. In fact, in our semiannual assessment of our core values, we decided as a team to add the core value of transparency, as we believed that being straight with our team, with our clients, and with the world would lead to greater trust. We ended up having a very productive two-day management session as we all addressed the brutal facts of our situation and made plans to emerge stronger than ever before.

Still, after the session the task of delivering the bad news to a wider audience—the company—remained. At that time there were thirty-eight employees, and we knew we'd have to cut five, a significant number. Letting people go is by far the toughest part of being a leader, and it was extremely difficult to execute this plan. But sure enough, the team understood and even appreciated how transparent we were throughout the process and how determined we were to remain transparent from then on.

In fact, we promised to put our business plan up on the walls of the office, and just days later we did just that. Now, six years and two companies later, we still have all company business plans up on the walls of our offices for employees, visitors, and even the janitors to see. I have come to believe that as important as positivity is, transparency builds trust, and trust is an essential asset for any team.

likeable local

One-Page Strategic Plan

Opportunities to exceed plan

Threats to making plan

CORE VALUES/BELIEFS (Should/Shouldn't)	PURPOSE (Why?)	TARGETS (3-5 YRS.) (Where)	GOALS (1 YR.) (What)
We are passionate about small business.	To empower small businesses to become more successful.	Future Date 12/31/17	Yr. Ending 12/31/15
Our customer's success is our success.	Actions: To Live Values, Purpose, BHAG	Run Rate $21M; NCLTV $7,100; Customers; Rev/Employee $140K; Monthly Revenue Churn 1.02%	Run Rate $4.5M; NCLTV $4,900; Customers; Rev/Employee $100K; Monthly Revenue Churn 2%
Always be improving.	1 Build & constantly improve industry leading product (HM/DL)	Sandbox: The most intelligent social media software for SMBs	Key Initiatives
Our work is fun.	2 Partner with the best global channels (DK/HM)	Key Thrusts/Capabilities, 3-5 Year priorities: 1 Improve ROI producing social/mobile web product (HM, DL)	Annual Priorities: 1 Fund, recruit, hire & lead 10+ animals (DK, MR, SS)
We're driven to create a #LikeableWorld.	3 Be the thought leader in social media use for SMBs (DK/NK/LM)	2 Launch & grow frictionless product line (DL, NK)	2 Launch & grow frictionless VIP product w/ 2k customers (DL, NK)
	4 Be the employer of choice (All)	3 Fund, recruit, hire, lead 100+ animals (DK, All)	3 Improve core product to drive 1st conversions for 90% of CGO (HM, DL)
	5 Scale our customer base quickly & thoughtfully (GP/LM)	4 Build & grow sales & CST model to create negative rev. churn (GP, LM)	4 Build & grow sales/CST model to create 2% for churn & become profitable (GP, LM, SS)
		5 Partner w 10 new orgs per year (DK, MR, NK)	5 Partner w 10 new orgs (DK, MR, NK)
	BHAG: Likeable Businesses on every Main Street.	KPI/Smart Numbers	1 or 2 Critical #s: Rev Run Rate: $4.5M; Mo Rev Churn: 2%
		Brand Promise/Overt Benefit: Build, engage, & grow your business using Social Media	

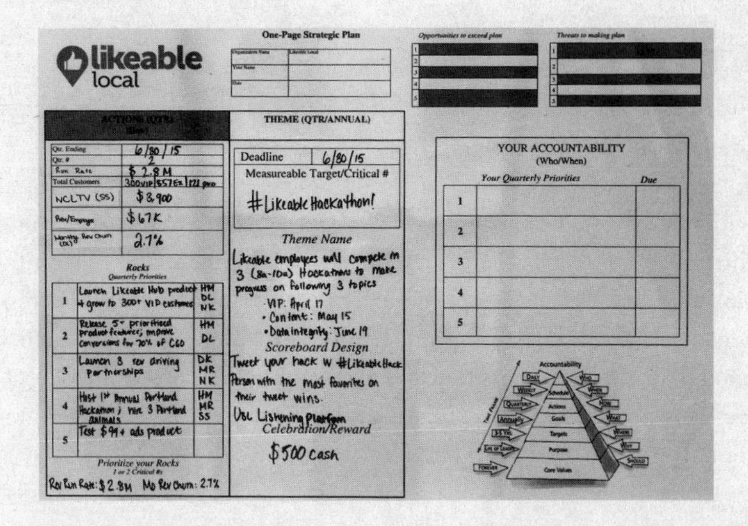

likeable local

One-Page Strategic Plan

Organization Name	Likeable Local
Your Name	
Date	

Opportunities to exceed plan: 1, 2, 3, 4, 5

Threats to making plan: 1, 2, 3, 4, 5

ACTIONS (QTR)

Qtr. Ending	6/30/15
Qtr. #	2
Run Rate	$2.8M
Total Customers	300 VIP / 557 Ex / 121 pro
NCLTV (SS)	$3,900
Rev/Employee	$67K
Monthly Rev Churn (DL)	2.7%

Rocks
Quarterly Priorities

1	Launch Likeable Hub product + grow to 300+ VIP customers	HM DL NK
2	Release 5+ prioritized product features; improve conversions for 70% of C60	HM DL
3	Launch 3 rev driving partnerships	DK MR NK
4	Host 1st Annual Portland Hackathon; hire 3 Portland animals	HM MR SS
5	Test $99+ ads product	

Prioritize your Rocks
1 or 2 Critical #s
Rev Run Rate: $2.8M Mo Rev Churn: 2.7%

THEME (QTR/ANNUAL)

Deadline	6/30/15

Measureable Target/Critical #
#LikeableHackathon!

Theme Name
Likeable employees will compete in 3 (8a-10a) Hackathons to make progress on following 3 topics
- VIP: April 17
- Content: May 15
- Data integrity: June 19

Scoreboard Design
Tweet your hack w #LikeableHack
Person with the most favorites on their tweet wins.
Use Listening Platform

Celebration/Reward
$500 cash

YOUR ACCOUNTABILITY
(Who/When)

	Your Quarterly Priorities	*Due*
1		
2		
3		
4		
5		

This advice to always share bad news might seem to contradict the advice I gave in the chapters about spreading positivity, but in reality these two ideas go hand in hand. Why? Well, people like to be around you when times are good, but for you to truly wield influence, you need people to want to be around you when times are not so good. No matter how positive and fantastic you are, there surely will be some bad times to weather. When you're going through those times, you'll need your team by your side. If you can be transparent with them, they'll know that what they see is what they get, and they'll trust you and continue to fight the good fight with you.

Delivering the brutal facts and laying off five employees at Likeable Media was extremely difficult. Fully embracing transparency wasn't much easier. But I know today that the trust built from the transparency was vital in growing the team and the company. In the end, we straightened the ship, doubled in size, and continued to grow, and that felt simply fantastic.

FAST First Action Steps to Take:

1. Do an inventory of how transparent you are with your direct reports and colleagues at work and your family at home.
2. Write down three brutal facts that you can share with your team or family in the spirit of transparency to help engender trust.
3. Deliver the transparent truth, but remain positive and steadfast in your determination to accomplish your vision.

39. Get High Before Every Meeting

"Why am I always so negative?" Andy wondered aloud to me.

I was coaching Andy for a presentation to our Entrepreneurs' Organization forum, and he was very upset. Andy is a fantastic real estate entrepreneur, a great father, and one of my closest friends. But he was right: He was often a negative thinker. We weren't sure exactly why he could be such a downer, but we were both determined to help him become more positive. Then Andy came up with an excellent idea.

"I read that gratitude is a powerful way of changing your mindset," he said, and it turns out that many great leaders have discovered the benefits of actively practicing gratitude: Cary Chessick, the founder and former CEO of Restaurant.com, used to motivate himself by writing out five things he was grateful for each day. Shawn Achor, a speaker and the author of the bestseller *The Happiness Advantage*, practices acts of gratitude every day to help train his brain to see the world in a more positive frame. Sheldon Yellen, the CEO of the billion-dollar company BELFOR, wrote of his habit of sending multiple thank-you/birthday cards to his employees every day. Srikumar Rao, "the happiness guru," author, and Columbia Business School professor, has written about the joy of having thoughts of gratitude each night before going to bed.

"These supersuccessful guys must be doing something right," Andy said. Thus began our work in helping Andy become more grateful in order to become more positive at work and in life. Over the course of the next several weeks, Andy developed a routine to incorporate acts of gratitude and kindness into his life. Using me as his accountability partner, he began writing down and emailing me who and what he was grateful for, as well as random acts of kindness he had performed each day.

At first my role in Andy's self-improvement project was that of coach, someone to guide him and keep him accountable, but a funny thing happened: As Andy's gratitude was quickly making him a happier and more positive person, I began to get awfully jealous. Now, to be honest, I've never really suffered from negative thinking, as so many people around me have. But nonetheless, I was envious of what Andy was getting out of the practice of gratitude. At the same time, I was inspired.

Under the pretense of supporting my friend Andy in his mission, I began to practice gratitude. I started by writing handwritten thank you cards, first one a week, then one a day, and then three per day, in the morning on my commute to work. I soon found that if I was in a bad mood, the act of feeling grateful made me feel better. I found that if I was already in a good mood, the act of gratitude made me feel great. And I found that if I was in a great mood, the act of experiencing gratitude made me feel ecstatic. I was feeling better than I had in ages and wanted more, and so I decided that my whole family would share each night at the dinner table one person we were grateful for that day. This, too, felt great and, as if I were an addict searching for a better and better high, left me wanting even more. Finally, I adopted Srikumar's practice of thinking grateful thoughts each night in bed just before I went to sleep.

I'll let you in on a little secret: For better or for worse, I've never done drugs. (To be clear, I'm no angel; it's just that drinking and gambling were my vices of choice in my wayward youth.) However, although I don't know what it feels like to be high on hard drugs, I do know that the high I get from gratitude is amazing. It's so good that I now choose to take a hit whenever it's convenient. If I'm about to give an important speech to my team, I'll write a thank you card.

If I've got a huge meeting with investors coming up, I'll list four or five things I'm grateful for. If I had a particularly rough day, I'll be sure to go to sleep feeling as grateful as possible.

Remember those mirror neurons from Chapter 36? Your gratefulness affects your mood in a positive way, which in turn affects the people you're leading and the people around you. As you go about your day, each meeting and even each interaction you have can be a positive one, filled with vision and hope and contagious gratitude, if you embrace it as such.

Thanks to the leaders I've mentioned—Cary Chessick, Shawn Achor, Sheldon Yellen, and Srikumar Rao—and thanks to Andy Cohen and the coaching work I did with him, I literally get high on gratitude every day. And for that I'm grateful.

FAST **F**irst **A**ction **S**teps to **T**ake:

1. Choose one of the gratitude activities in this chapter and write down your plan for making it happen in your life.
2. Put your gratitude plan into action. Start small and work your way up, as making any habit routine is challenging. The good news is that if it's as addictive for you as it's been for me, you'll be practicing more gratitude in no time.
3. The next time you're feeling down about something, try putting it aside for a moment and writing a thank you card to someone. It might transform your mood in an instant.

40. Everybody Wants to Be a Leader

"Now, David, you can be a leader no matter what. Make the right choice."

When I was in first grade, I always wanted to be the class line leader. I would fuss and sometimes even get into mischief when I wasn't. But then my teacher, Mrs. Flayton, at Public School 230 in Brooklyn, New York, would say to me, as she often said to the whole class, "David, you can be a leader no matter what."

What she meant was that even if we weren't the line leader that day, we could all set a good example for others and guide them to do the right thing, and those things were what made a true leader—regardless of who had been chosen that day to walk at the head of the line. Mrs. Flayton didn't just speak those words; she drilled them into us all: *You can be a leader no matter what.* She did such an excellent job of imparting that lesson that eventually everyone in our first-grade class came to believe that in one way or another we could all become leaders.

It was a powerful, moving thought: Who wouldn't want to consider himself a leader, after all? Given the choice between being a leader and being a follower, I think we'd all choose to be a leader, at least in our own heads.

Thirty years later, after having led two companies and, more important, a family, and after writing about leadership in several books and magazines, I find that those words from Mrs. Flayton resonate with me as much as ever. The truth, I've realized, is that not only can everybody *become* a leader, most people, if not all people, want to be *thought of* as a leader in one way or another. And as I learned way back in the first grade, those who think of themselves as a leader are more likely to behave like one.

As a leader yourself, you have an opportunity to inspire leadership of all kinds in your team. As always, your team doesn't have to mean your company, and you don't have to be a CEO. It can mean your small project team at work or even your family at home. How can you inspire leadership from the ranks, so to speak? Assign as many leaders as possible. Be generous with praise for their leadership abilities and, to the extent possible, hold up each leadership position as honorable and desirable.

For example, at home, my wife and I used this tactic to get our daughter, Charlotte, to take her chores more seriously. Instead of ordering (or begging) her to clear the table, we appointed her "president of table clearing" and gave her the distinction and honor of such a duty. From then on she happily and proudly cleared the table every single night. I've also implemented more or less the same strategy at our companies, where we've been generous with titles and subsequently probably have more vice presidents than most companies of a similar size. But so what? Leadership titles are free to give out and make people feel good. Why shouldn't you be blessed with as many leaders as possible on your team?

If everybody wants to feel like a leader, surely you can find a way to make that happen.

Mrs. Flayton sure did. Back in first grade we didn't just have line leaders. We also had homework leaders, bathroom pass leaders, activity leaders, and chalkboard leaders. Everybody felt ownership of something, responsibility for something, and pride in something. She assigned leadership roles for every chore that had to get done in class, and in the same way you can create as many leaders as you want for the various tasks that need to get done. This will give people a greater sense of ownership, responsibility, pride, and commitment, making them more likely to deliver the results that you want.

I feel blessed to have written one of the most popular leadership articles ever on LinkedIn, "11 Simple Concepts to Become a Better Leader." To date, nearly three million people have chosen to read this article, indicating to me just how many people want to become better leaders no matter what their role is today. I am certain that as social media continues to make the world more transparent, the hierarchical barrier of leadership will fade away. These days, anyone can be a leader, whether the group you're leading is your company, your team, your department, or your family. You can be a leader even if you have no official leadership role and are simply setting a good example for the people around you. I am certain as ever that as Mrs. Flayton told a bunch of five- and six-year-olds, *You can be a leader no matter what.*

And you can develop many leaders on your team as well.

FAST First Action Steps to Take:

1. Make a list of the people on your team and possible leadership roles for each one. Think of creative ways to describe their leadership roles.
2. Assign new leadership roles for the people on your team. If it's feasible, consider new titles for people as well.
3. As you grow in your own role as a leader, consider the ways in which everyone wants to be a leader and give everyone a chance to be one.

9

Resolving Conflict with People

41. If You're There to Help, You're There to Win

"I've been maced, I've been maced!" I shouted from the second-floor hallway of my high school.

I was scared and confused and pretty angry. What had begun as an innocent dispute with my friend Al Fins over our simulated baseball dice game in the spring of my junior year at Hunter College High School had deteriorated into a terrible situation. Al and I had trusted in the strength of our friendship and had chosen to share control of one team in this game we played, which is called Pursue the Pennant. (For the uninitiated, imagine the role-playing game Dungeons & Dragons meets fantasy baseball.)

Anyway, it turned out that this faith had not been entirely warranted. Al and I had gotten into a disagreement that prompted him to seize the "team" from me (i.e., he took the twenty-five playing cards that made up the team and refused to share them with me). Now, I have never been a bully or even aggressive in any way, but I happened to be one of the biggest, tallest people in the eleventh grade at Hunter, and Al happened to be one of the smallest. When I approached Al in the hallway to get back my team, he must have felt quite threatened. He also must have been prepared, because before I could get near him, he whipped out a can of Mace and sprayed me in the face.

Moments later I was screaming and didn't know what to do. A friend suggested that I go to the school nurse, and I did. The nurse flushed my eyes out with water and cleared me to go back to class.

Unfortunately, before I could do that, I had to make a mandatory stop at the vice principal's office, where Ms. Gemmola and Al Fins, the Mace perpetrator, were waiting for me. Even though I thought I had been the victim, I knew that I wasn't completely innocent, and I certainly didn't want to get in trouble, and so when I walked into Ms.

Gemmola's office, I was fully prepared and expected to have to defend myself.

You can imagine how startled I was when Ms. Gemmola began the conversation: "Now, boys, please know one thing. I'm here to help you. Whether or not you walk out of this room with suspension or other consequences, please know that above all else, I am here to help."

In a strange way, that statement put me at ease. On one hand, I was nervous about her use of the word *suspension*. I had never been suspended from school, and I certainly didn't want the first time to be on the same day I'd been maced.

On the other hand, Ms. Gemmola had said (twice even) that she was there to help. If I trusted her, I should feel safe. After all, I was just trying to resolve a conflict with Al about our PtP baseball team, and things had escalated out of control. Obviously we needed some help to resolve our disagreement.

Still, I was a sixteen-year-old kid and not as seasoned as I am today, and so I replied: "Help me? I've been maced!"

"Well, I'm sure there was a reason Al felt so threatened by you," Ms Gemmola responded. "Let's do this. I'd love to hear both sides of the story, and then, as I said, once I've listened thoroughly to both of you, I'll help you come to a resolution. Of course, as a representative of the school, I need to help come up with a fair resolution as well."

Al gave his side of the story first and in fact did say he thought I was going to attack him and thought the only way he could protect himself was with Mace. I then admitted that I might have been physically imposing but said (truthfully) that I had never intended to lay a hand on Al: I just wanted my team back.

In the end, Ms. Gemmola brokered a deal that left everyone as happy as possible. I agreed not to get Al in trouble for macing me, and in exchange he would give my team cards back and agree to let me finish the season on my own. Neither of us would be suspended or otherwise punished for the incident, said Ms. Gemmola, but it would be noted, and if either of us had any more issues with each other or anyone else, we would definitely face a suspension from school. It was a win-win outcome for both of us.

As a school administrator, Ms. Gemmola truly *was* there to help us, and it showed. Resolving conflicts with others is no easy task. But the moral of this story is that if you take the attitude of being there to *help*, you can always find a way for all parties to win.

In Chapter 17, we talked about how the most important question in starting a new relationship with someone is "How can I help you?" In resolving conflicts with others, the most important question to ask is "How can I help resolve this in a way that leaves all parties happy?" Although it's true that finding the answer to the second question often will involve some give-and-take and compromise, it's much easier if you take the attitude of "How can I help?" versus "How can I punish?" or "How can I be right?" or "How can I show them?" Part of "How can I help?" is always "How can I help you feel heard?" and as you'll remember from earlier chapters, few things are more effective in gaining respect and influence than making others feel heard.

Your attitude toward resolving a conflict, whether it's a conflict between you and someone else or a conflict between two other people, makes all the difference. Going in looking to help people puts both parties at ease to the greatest extent possible. It also sets up a journey toward an outcome that everyone can live with: In any conflict, all we want is to feel heard and be helped and have the issue resolved.

When Al and I calmed down that day, we realized that this was actually a great solution for everyone involved, and we were thankful for the outcome. I finished our season on my own, and though I lost, I appreciated Ms. Gemmola for being there to help.

Twenty years later, I'm still playing the Pursue the Pennant role-playing baseball game with my friends. It's probably my favorite hobby outside of family and work. Who knows if I'd still be playing if Ms. Gemmola hadn't helped me get my cards back from Al Fins that day?

FAST First Action Steps to Take:

1. Describe a recent conflict you've had. Imagine how you might have resolved the conflict better if you had taken the approach of "How can I help both parties?"
2. Write down an action plan for how you will deal with the next conflict with that person with more of an eye to helping the other party feel heard and resolved.
3. Put the action plan into effect the next time you have a conflict. Remember, if you're there to help, you're there to win.

42. Let Cooler Heads Prevail

NOOOOOOOO!" I screamed, and slammed the door on my way out. I was angry at my wife and felt so out of control. I just wanted a little space, and so I left the house in anger.

It had all begun with a friendly family game of Clue. Everything had been going well until I made a guess at "whodunit" and was wrong. Turned out that it was only because my ten-year-old daughter, Charlotte, had accidentally given me some misinformation, but it didn't matter because once you make an accusation in Clue and are wrong, you're out of the game. As a supercompetitive player, I was very upset about being eliminated and sure that it was my daughter's fault.

Obviously, soon thereafter, I realized that it was only a game and an innocent mistake by my very young daughter and not a big deal. But at the time I was really caught up in the game and upset with the outcome. When my wife, Carrie, said, "Don't blame Charlotte; it's your fault for being wrong," I totally lost control of myself. I'm embarrassed to admit it, but it's true: I tried to excuse myself politely from the kids and proceeded to storm out of the house in a rage.

What made things worse was that my wife insisted on trying to resolve the conflict right away. Just moments after I'd left the house, I got a text from her, then another, and then another.

"COME BACK TO THE HOUSE NOW!" the first message read. Over and over came messages demanding that I come back to the house and talk. Even though all I wanted at the time was space to cool down, in an effort to resolve the conflict (and probably because at some level I realized how in the wrong I was) I went back to the house to talk with my wife.

The problem was, I wasn't in the right mindset to resolve any conflict. Whether I was overreacting or not (I was), I was filled with rage. I felt out of control, I felt unsupported, and I felt unable to think and speak rationally. Thus, when my wife went on to lecture me on how wrong I was to erupt like that in front of the kids, though I didn't fight back (I knew better), it really wasn't a productive conversation. Though I was listening to her, I wasn't actively engaged in the conversation, and so I'm sure she wasn't getting much satisfaction out of it, either. Eventually, we went to sleep.

The next morning we had a better, much more productive conversation. I told her how out of control I had felt and, more important, how unsupported I had felt by her comments. She said that she heard me and understood but that I could never act out my rage like that in front of her or the kids and that it had really scared her. I felt horrible and embarrassed and apologized profusely. We made up and committed to each other and to ourselves and to our children. Most important, we agreed that when future conflicts arose, we would make sure to resolve them when both of our mindsets were right.

What was the difference between these conversations? In the first one, the previous night, I was still in a state of rage. In the second one, I was calm, cool, and rational, and that made all the difference. Essentially, it's impossible to resolve conflicts with someone in a state of rage or in any highly volatile emotional state, and so it's simply inadvisable to try. In such situations, no matter how much you want to resolve a conflict immediately, it's always best to wait until cooler heads prevail.

If you're the one who's in the emotionally volatile state, you've got to be able to articulate that—and only that—in a calm way. In other words, you've got to be able to say to the other party something like this: "I'm in a highly volatile state and would really appreciate trying to resolve this later." Admittedly, it's very hard to say this calmly while you're so worked up, but it's essential.

If you're the party who's dealing with someone in a highly emotional state, it's essential to give that person space before trying to resolve the conflict. As tempting as it might be to resolve things as soon as possible, it simply won't work until both parties are calm, cool, and collected. Don't waste any time and energy on the situation if you can see that the other person's emotions are still red hot. Instead, take a deep breath, give the other person space, and resolve the conflict later.

In so many interpersonal situations, time is a valuable asset. Conflict resolution, whether at home or at work, is one of them. Avoid the temptation to resolve things right away, and give the situation some time. Both parties probably will come back to the table calmer and more able to have a rational discussion that leaves everyone feeling better.

A few weeks later, we played another family game of Clue. This time, no matter whodunit, I was determined to remember it was only a game and, having dunit wrong before, to get things right this time. Technically my wife won that game, but really, we all won.

FAST First **A**ction **S**teps to **T**ake:

1. Come to a mutual understanding with your significant others at home and/or your close associates at work about the emotional state in which you will try to solve conflicts and the emotional state in which you will not. Articulate this understanding to one another.
2. When a conflict does arise, give each other some space to make sure nobody is trying to resolve the situation while feeling rage, being out of control, or experiencing other extremely volatile feelings.
3. Talk about and resolve the conflict after you've each had ample time to reflect, get calm, and get rational.
4. Reflect on the entire conflict-resolution process and how it can be improved further.

43. Let Go to Get What You Want

"This is impossible," I said to my psychotherapist, Judy, with despair. "She'll never leave her husband, and she'll never be with me."

I was an anxious mess. I was madly in love with her, my office co-worker at Radio Disney. Not only was I in love with her, I wanted—no, I *expected*—her to leave her husband for me. I knew she had feelings for me, but it was an impossible situation because despite my feelings for her and her feelings for me, she was married. Furthermore, she was a loyal and responsible wife, and even if she knew deep down she had married the wrong person, she was determined to do the right thing and try to make her marriage work.

"How can I make her leave her husband?" I asked Judy. I was used to getting what I wanted, and surely there was a way to do that in this situation.

"Can you do that?" Judy replied, answering a question with a question like the excellent therapist she was.

"Well," I reasoned. "I guess I can't make her do anything. God knows I've tried, and it doesn't seem to be working for me."

"What can you do, then?" Judy said. "What can you control in this uncontrollable conflict?"

I thought for a minute, and then I replied with what I thought was the right answer: "I guess I can control letting go of the situation."

"Exactly!" Judy said. "The solution to a conflict you simply cannot control is letting go: of control, of the outcome, of everything."

But of course that solution would be much easier said than done. The reality is that letting go is hard. In fact, the more you want something or someone, the harder it is to let go. Fortunately for me, Judy didn't stop there.

"What else can you control, Dave?" she said.

I scratched my head and thought about it a bit. It had been hard enough to think of letting go, and I sure as heck couldn't think of anything else I could control in this impossible situation. Finally, my therapist broke the silence.

"Can you control taking good care of yourself?" she asked. "Can you control eating well, exercising, getting enough sleep, and generally treating your body well?"

"Of course I can." I half shrugged and half smiled. I was annoyed, because I couldn't see how that would bring me any closer to getting what I wanted.

Judy was dead right, though. No matter how stressful the situation was, no matter how anxiety-producing and crazy-making the conflict was, no matter how much I felt that I had no choices at the time, the truth was that I did have choices. I could choose to let go, and I could choose to take great care of myself even in my darkest hour. It certainly wouldn't be easy, but I was in control.

Sometimes you can resolve conflicts with people easily. Sometimes it takes work, but through time and effort, through listening and mirroring and validation—along with a dose of patience—you can get to a good place with someone. But sometimes conflicts simply can't be solved. In those instances, the best way, really the only way, to resolve a conflict with another person is to decide to let go. Resolve to surrender what you can't control and to control what you always can: taking great care of your mind, body, and heart.

Alcoholics Anonymous has a prayer they say at every meeting that is simple but powerful:

God, grant me the serenity
To accept the things I cannot change,

The courage to change the things I can,
And the wisdom to know the difference.

Maybe your husband is cheating on you. Maybe your boss is mistreating you. Maybe the love of your life won't leave her husband for you. There are many conflicts that will arise between you and another person that you won't have control over. Often, the faster you can recognize that, let go, and move on or get out, the sooner you'll feel resolved.

It's not easy by any stretch of the imagination. Letting go of that married officemate was the hardest thing I've ever done. Letting go of the idea that she'd leave her husband for me was a constant battle for months. Ultimately, I took those words from Judy to heart: I focused on what I could control: I took care of myself, began exercising regularly, and went on a strict diet regimen that had me losing sixty-nine pounds and getting into the best shape of my life.

Each day it got a little easier to deal with accepting the fact that this was one conflict whose outcome I couldn't control. I knew I couldn't see her every day and still let go, and so I made the difficult decision to leave Disney, the company we worked at together, and cut off all communication between us.

Anything could have happened, but as you already know from the Introduction, this story had a happy ending. Over a year after I'd last talked to Carrie and months after I'd finally let her go, she became available. I cautiously chose to reengage with her at that time, and, well, ten years, one marriage, two businesses, and, most important, three children later, the rest is history.

Sometimes you have to learn to let go to get what you want.

FAST First **A**ction **S**teps to **T**ake:

1. Write down a time when you had to let go of a person, thought, or goal. How did it feel, and what did you do to make it work?
2. Write down a list of five ways you can make the choice to take better care of yourself in a time of conflict.
3. The next time a conflict arises that you deem unsolvable, refer back to these two items, work to let go, and make the positive choice to take care of yourself.

44. Put On a Bulletproof Vest (or the Simple System That Saved My Marriage)

I just can't take it anymore. Why can't we learn how to resolve conflicts better? We've been married for seven years! We're good at getting along, so why can't we get good at fighting? You'd think we'd have it down by now!"

My wife, Carrie, was angry and frustrated. Frankly, I was, too, because she was right. We had been married for seven years, and overall it had been seven wonderful ones. But our communication certainly could have used improvement, especially our communication when we fought. It just seemed like we repeated the same things over and over: I felt criticized, she felt unappreciated, I got angry and needed space, and she always wanted to talk about everything.

On one hand, we knew that every couple fights. On the other hand, we both wanted to learn to fight better, resolve conflicts better, and in general communicate better.

Several entrepreneur friends in New York swore by this one therapist, Dr. Bonnie, and so we decided to give her a try. Dr. Bonnie Weil is an accomplished psychologist, bestselling author, and thought leader in the psychology of relationships. She had appeared on countless television shows, including the *Oprah Winfrey Show*—five times—sharing her expertise. She was expensive but, according to my entrepreneur friends, well worth it, so we decide to pay her a visit.

Within one fifty-minute session, amazingly, it felt like Dr. Bonnie understood exactly where each of us was coming from and how we felt. More important, in just three sessions Dr. Bonnie gave us a system for resolving difficult conflicts that we've used successfully now for several years and through many an argument. You could even argue that it's saved our marriage.

Here's her system, as we practice it at least:

1. The person who's upset at the other person requests an appointment to discuss it and offers a few possible times to talk. Importantly, none of those times is "right now." This way, it gives that person some time and space to prepare.
2. When it's time for the appointment, the two people get together in a quiet, safe place, and the offending party agrees to put on a bulletproof vest. In other words, he agrees to not be offended or get defensive about what the other person is saying. Instead, he agrees to focus on listening and understanding.
3. The person who's upset describes the problem in its entirety and how it's making her feel.
4. The other person mirrors and validates everything his partner is saying, not trying to solve or defend or do anything but listen, mirror, and validate.
5. The offending party offers a genuine, authentic "I'm sorry."
6. When both parties agree that the offended party feels heard and understood, that person shares three possible positive solutions to the problem. The offending party agrees to at least one of the solutions.
7. Finally and perhaps most important, both people celebrate the successful resolution of the conflict by engaging in physical activity together. Sure, that could mean going for a jog, but if that physical activity happens to be intimate, it's even better!

You might be thinking that this system seems awfully forced and even robotic, and I think that's a fair complaint about it. But that being said, it really does work. Here's an example of Bonnie's system in action:

One day a year or so ago, I was taking the train home with my wife after work, and Carrie asked me why I hadn't fired an employee yet whom I knew I had to fire. I felt criticized and angry at her for bringing it up the way she did, and I felt out of control and trapped to be on the train with her while experiencing those emotions. I told Carrie I was upset and wanted an appointment and offered her three possible times to discuss it.

Carrie took the earliest appointment, and a couple of hours later we sat down together in our bedroom. Carrie put on her bulletproof vest, and I shared what I was upset about. Carrie did a great job of listening, mirroring, and validating how I was feeling. She said, "I'm sorry," and I knew she meant it. Then I suggested three possible solutions: We could choose not to discuss work on the train, we could choose to not take the train together anymore, or we could have a code word for when a sensitive topic came up in conversation while we were on the train together.

Carrie said she really loved taking the train with me and wanted to be able to keep doing it, so she chose the first solution: We no longer would talk about work on the train (she also said we should use the third solution in case we ever broke that plan and the conversation got out of hand). We closed the conversation with some jumping jacks, which, to be honest, were followed by much more intimate physical activity. Suffice it to say that soon enough we both felt much better.

Most important, since then, we have barely talked about work on the train, and we haven't had another argument like that again. In the long run, it really worked!

Obviously, this system is more appropriate for conflicts at home with your significant other than for conflicts at work (especially step 7). But if it is used in the appropriate setting, it's simple and truly effective. I'm thankful to Dr. Bonnie for sharing it with me and hopeful that you can solve a problem or two with the one you love as well.

FAST First **A**ction **S**teps to **T**ake:

1. Write down the name of your significant other or the person you're closest with and then write down a recent conflict you've had with that person.
2. Using Dr. Bonnie's system, write down how you might have resolved that conflict better.
3. Share this chapter with your partner and agree to use this system to resolve your next conflict.
4. The next time you have a conflict with your significant other, refer back to this system and give it a try. Even if it feels forced, stiff, or robotic, see it through. You might be surprised and delighted with the results.

10

Inspiring People

45. Remember That It's Not About You

"Why the hell am I so nervous?" I wondered. It was moments before I would get up to speak to an audience of three thousand people in Mexico City at an entrepreneurship conference. But despite the many people who would be hanging on my every word, I wasn't sure why I was so nervous. Usually, the larger the crowd, the more excited I got, not the more nervous.

Right before I took the stage, my entrepreneur/speaker/author friend Mike Michalowicz, who was up after me, approached me. I thought he could sense my nerves.

"Big crowd, eh?" Mike said. I nodded in agreement, and then Mike shared with me an important lesson that has stuck with me ever since.

"Remember," he said. "It's all about them, not you. Inspiring your audience is all about helping them see their own vision, not yours."

This may seem simplistic, but it's absolutely critical advice for anyone trying to inspire others, whether it's from the stage at a large conference; in a meeting with a boss, team, or department; on a client pitch or sales call; or at home with one's spouse and kids. The bottom line is that like it or not, people don't really care about you, certainly not the way they care about themselves, their families, and their close friends. Think about it: You're reading this book so that you can improve your communication and people skills, but you don't really care about me, Dave, except for how I can help you. And that's okay!

Whether you're speaking to an audience of three thousand, three hundred, thirty, or three, if your hope is to inspire them, your material and delivery have to be about them and how they can grow, not about you.

Inspiring your audience is all about **helping them** see **their own vision**, not yours.

This doesn't mean you can't tell stories about yourself, share things you've learned, or talk about your products, services, features, and benefits. All those things are fair game and often are very helpful in delivering an inspiring presentation; storytelling in particular is a great way to make a lesson or message come alive. But as you tell stories, do a product demo, or talk about your company, it's essential that you paint a picture of what *your audience's* life looks like now and what they want it to look like in the future. Even more important, it's essential to show how whatever you're selling—whether it's a product, idea, message, or pure inspiration—fits in with their vision of a better future.

People like hearing success stories. But you know what they like more? Their own success stories. If you want to inspire (and perhaps sell something along the way), you'll want to get people thinking about themselves and their future selves.

It's easy to get caught in the trap of thinking it's about you or your product. If you're a salesperson or an entrepreneur or a leader of any kind, the spotlight is often on you and/or the product you sell. But no matter how much the spotlight is on you, it's essential to stay humble and keep the conversation about the other person or people in the room, not about you.

This is especially valuable as both a mindset and a tool in creating presentations. For instance, if you're doing a sales presentation, the slides should remind your audience what their problem is and how your solution will alleviate it. It should help them imagine and even envision life without that problem.

Even if you're not a public speaker by profession, you're probably in the business of inspiring someone in one area or another in your work. Certainly, all salespeople and marketers are. Entrepreneurs, engineers, and designers need to inspire with their products. Anyone who's a manager needs to inspire her team to be more productive. Even parenting is all about inspiring one's children. Whenever you aim to inspire, it's helpful to remind yourself that it's not about you.

When Mike Michalowicz shared that lesson with me, it was perfect timing. I was about to tell my story to three thousand people, and although I'm sure they would have found it interesting, I'm happy he said what he did, because not only did he put me at ease, he helped shape a much better keynote speech. Instead of making it about me, I made the entire speech about my audience, mostly entrepreneurs, and how they could grow their businesses.

Today, whether I'm speaking to thousands of people or just a few, I often say those words to myself right before it's time to present: "It's not about you."

FAST First **A**ction **S**teps to **T**ake:

1. Write down the names of the people you want to inspire at work and at home.
2. For all those people, write down what you think their vision of themselves is in six months, one year, and three years. If you're not sure, ask them.
3. The next time you prepare to speak to them, remind yourself what their vision of themselves is and how whatever you are selling can help them achieve that vision. Then use that to frame your remarks.
4. Every time you speak or present to a new audience, remember that *it's not about you.*

46. Be Unoriginal, Part 1: You Can Quote Me on This

I felt speechless.

I was about to address our team at Likeable Media and share some really big news: I was leaving the company to start a new one, Likeable Local, and my wife, Carrie, was going to take over as CEO of Likeable Media. I knew that this news would be seen as a big deal by some of the staff, and I was searching for the perfect way to word it. But I was coming up short.

"What should I say?" I asked my entrepreneur friend Jeff. "I'm really struggling with how to talk about embracing change."

"Don't say anything original," Jeff replied, prompting me to scratch my head in confusion. "Whatever you want to say has been said before better than you can say it and by someone way more successful than you."

I still felt confused and perhaps a little insulted, but I thought I understood what he meant.

"In other words . . ." I began to say.

"Exactly," Jeff said. "In other words. As in, in another's words. As in, use a quote to open the meeting and help people embrace what it is you want to say."

I thought this concept was smart and at least worth a little research. I thanked Jeff and dashed to my computer and Googled "inspirational quotes about change."

I was amazed with the results, of which there were over 32 million. I began to click around and found literally dozens of quotes that inspired me and that I knew could inspire our team to accept the big change I was about to announce. I settled on a quote from Benjamin Franklin and went back to preparing for the meeting.

Later, I got to thinking. Jeff was right that Ben Franklin and many others had said exactly what I wanted to say before and had said it way better than I ever could, not only about change but about pretty much everything. I wasn't insulted by this. In fact, it made sense: There truly is very little original thought left out there, so why shouldn't we take advantage of the brilliant minds of the past and borrow the words they used to convey ideas and inspire others? In another person's words, why reinvent the wheel?

I continued my research and ended up with over four hundred inspirational quotes that I loved on over thirty different topics I cared about: listening, storytelling, authenticity, and gratefulness, to name a few. The quotes came from a wide variety of sources, from presidents to movie stars, authors to business leaders, athletes to poets. What they had in common was how powerfully and effectively they summed up an idea I might want to address or a message I wanted to send. More important, all the quotes inspired me, and so I figured they could inspire others as well. (See Appendix B for some of those quotes.)

I began using quotes in my team meetings at work and in sales meetings as well. I continued to research quotes and became obsessed with the idea of finding the perfect quote to match what I wanted to say at any specific time.

Of course, a quote alone would not suffice; I still had to add some of my own words into the mix. But I found that opening (and sometimes closing) a meeting with an inspirational quote was a great way to inspire my team, get alignment, and prepare people for what was to come. It got easier and easier to find and use quotes, and I ended up using them not only in meetings but in my own social media content. In fact, some of my most popular, retweeted, and reshared content ever has been quotes from other people.

You might think this is lazy or unoriginal. Some might even think it's unethical. But I believe that as long as you properly credit your source each time you share a quote, it's not only ethical but powerful, inspirational, and helpful to share quotes both across social media and face-to-face.

People love a little inspiration whether it's morning, noon, or night. If you can find a quote from someone else who says what you're thinking or feeling succinctly and powerfully, by all means consider sharing that quote (with credit) with your team and with the world.

That meeting with the Likeable Media team went quite well, and it was the first of many successful meetings I would open and/or close with a quote. My social media following has increased dramatically since I started tweeting and sharing quotes, and though it's impossible to show causation, it's easy to show a correlation between when I started sharing quotes and when my social media following took off.

I'll close with the quote that inspired my team that day and started it all:

> When you're finished changing, you're finished.
>
> —Benjamin Franklin

FAST **F**irst **A**ction **S**teps to **T**ake:

1. Review the quotes in Appendix B and note the ones that inspire you and the ones that you may want to share in social media and face-to-face with your team.
2. Research inspirational quotes about the topics you find yourself talking about at work and at home. Collect a list of your own quotes that you can use to inspire others.
3. Experiment with using quotes in social media and to open and/or close meetings at work. Remember always to acknowledge the quote's source.

47. Homelessness: The Instant Cure for Any Bad Mood

I was going through a very tough week as a leader.

One of my companies had an extremely toxic employee I had had to let go the previous Friday. And throughout the week, I was traveling constantly—from New York to Portland, Maine, on Monday; Boston on Wednesday; and Washington, D.C., on Thursday.

By midday Thursday, I was physically and emotionally exhausted. I was really hungry, too, and so when I had a little extra time before my afternoon meeting in Washington, I looked up the best sushi place in town on Yelp. After walking nearly a mile to get there (the reviews were really good), I arrived at the sushi joint only to find a sign that said "Closed this week for renovations."

At that point, I lost control of my emotions and actually shed some tears. I was so tired, so hungry, and so stressed. Determined not to be defeated, I began walking toward my next meeting, on the lookout for a place to get a quick bite to eat on the way. That was when a homeless man on the street interrupted my walk, asking, "May I have a quarter to get something to eat?"

Typically, I don't stop when people ask for money on the street. It's not that I don't care; it's just that I prefer to make donations to organizations that distribute food and provide shelter. But this time, for some reason, I stopped and searched my pants for some change. I couldn't find any, so I decided to reach for my wallet to grab a dollar instead.

"I swear, I don't drink or get high, sir," said the man, perhaps sensing that he was going to get more than just change. "I could really just use a dollar to get a sandwich."

I didn't have any one-dollar bills in my wallet and didn't want to stiff the guy, so I took out a twenty-dollar bill and handed it to the man.

"Oh, Jesus," he exclaimed. "God bless you! Thank you so much, sir!" he added, and I went on my way.

Then something crazy happened. My bad mood just melted away. I couldn't believe how much better I felt instantly. I had gone from feeling depressed, exhausted, overwhelmed, and stressed out to feeling blessed, fortunate, happy, and high on life in a matter of seconds and at a remarkably low cost of $20. Although some would argue that giving money to someone on the street is a selfless act, I would argue that I got plenty out of it, too, in terms of how great it made me feel and how incredibly quickly it transformed my mood.

A random act of kindness is an instant cure for any bad mood. You don't have to give $20 to a man on the street. You can pick up litter. You can call your grandma. You can hold the door for the next ten people to come and go from your office building. You can retweet a bunch of random people trying to promote something.

You can do anything that takes you out of yourself and, if only for a moment, focuses your time and attention completely on someone needier than you in one way or another. This is at once both a selfless act and a selfish one, because no matter what, you'll feel better after being kind. Then you'll be more prepared to be the best leader you can be and take on the world and its challenges.

In Chapter 36, I talked about mirror neurons and the power of your mood to affect others. The bottom line is that there will be many times when you're not in the mood to inspire others. But as a leader, you can't afford to have too many of those times, and you can't afford to fake it, either. That's where this method comes in handy. Whether you give $20 to a homeless person or commit another random act of kindness, you can and will instantly transform your mood *and* put yourself in a better position to inspire and persuade others.

A random act of kindness is an instant cure for any bad mood.

That day, I went on to have two very productive meetings in Washington, D.C., one of which resulted in landing a big new client, and then returned home feeling refreshed and recommitted to leading two companies. I felt like I could take on the world. And it only cost me twenty bucks.

FAST First Action Steps to Take:

1. Make a list of random acts of kindness that can be done near your office or home.
2. The next time you are in a bad mood about something (maybe a rejection, an unkind word from a boss or client, or something personal), take a ten-minute break and go out and perform one act of kindness (or more).
3. Note your mood before and after the act of kindness. Continue experimenting until you find an act of kindness that you can repeat as needed. Think of random acts of kindness as an inexhaustible resource you can tap into anywhere, any time.

48. Don't Let One Unkind Word Destroy Years of Praise

"Nicky, you're getting lazy," I chastised. "You used to be our top sales guy, and now you're barely making quota. Get your act together."

As soon as I had uttered those words, I realized I had made a grave mistake. Nicky had in fact been the top salesperson at Likeable Local for nearly two years. He had contributed a ton to the company, and as its leader, I had praised him generously and publicly throughout those two years.

But Nicky *had* been getting lazy lately, and his performance had slowed down a lot. Still, the moment I criticized him in front of his peers, I knew I had erred. To make amends, I privately messaged Nicky and set up a one-on-one meeting at which I walked through his history with the company, reminding him of his many highlights and imploring him to return to his previously solid form. I also apologized profusely for calling him out in front of his coworkers. But it was too late. The damage had been done.

People love praise. You can never praise people too much. When you are leading or inspiring a team, your number one resource is praise, not just for your top people but for anyone and everyone who demonstrates success in any task, no matter how small. Praise makes people feel good. It reverberates across a room. It makes a person singled out feel special and honored and excited and makes everyone else in the room want to emulate that person. Whether you are managing a team at work or children at home, praise is powerful, contagious, and totally inspirational.

Criticism has exactly the opposite effect on people. Criticism, especially public criticism, makes people feel embarrassed, afraid, and even humiliated. It makes the person who is singled out feel bad and everyone else in the room feel sad or scared. Although some leaders, including sales managers, football coaches, and even some parents, still try to motivate or inspire with criticism, that group and that method are dwindling as a mountain of research demonstrates the ill effects of that misguided approach.

Sometimes public criticism does have a seemingly positive short-term impact. Take a sales floor, for instance. If a sales manager barks, "Dave, why aren't you on the phones selling? Get back on the phones before you lose your job!" the rest of the sales team surely will take notice and probably jump on the phones and be more productive . . . for the next five or ten minutes. But the longer-term effects are deleterious. How? Dave will feel embarrassed and may start looking for another job in which he won't feel embarrassed. The others in the room will feel scared and also may start looking for another job in which they won't feel scared. For a few extra phone calls and maybe a few extra sales, you risk hurting and even losing your team in the long run. Fear, embarrassment, and shame are never inspirational beyond a very short time window.

When I studied teaching, I remember learning about the effects of positive praise on children. I brought that learning into my classroom and was amazed by the results. Instead of telling kids to quiet down or yelling or complaining at the ones who weren't listening or following directions, I singled out with praise the children who were following directions well ("I like the way Amy is sitting at her desk ready to learn!"). Incredibly, this method nearly always worked. Others wanted my praise, whether consciously or not, and acted accordingly to earn it.

The reality is that sometimes people need constructive criticism to improve. Sometimes people can truly benefit from feedback from you, but it's important to remember that nobody likes to be criticized. Even people who say they're good at accepting feedback surely would rather be praised than criticized.

Therefore, it's essential when you are delivering criticism, whether to an employee, a vendor, a partner, a family member, or anyone else, to do it carefully and thoughtfully. Here's a quick guide to giving feedback effectively:

1. *Never* give out criticism in front of other people. It never works. (It only leads to shame and fear.)
2. Instead, set up a time to have a one-on-one private discussion with the person with whom you want to share feedback.
3. Offer up a "praise sandwich": Start with something you like about the person and/or the job he's doing, continue with the negative feedback, and close by affirming how much you value the person and how confident you are in him.
4. Make sure to offer positive solutions to the issues at hand and get alignment on the solution of choice.
5. Don't dwell on the negative, and look for future opportunities to publicly praise the positive about the person as soon and as much as you can.

Giving constructive criticism can be difficult for you, but think of it this way: It's always more difficult to receive feedback than to give it. However, giving public praise is easy, contagious, fun, and totally inspiring for you, for the person receiving it, and even for the others around you who inevitably will be motivated and energized by it. Even in a tough situation, you can capitalize on just one person doing just one little thing well and quickly and powerfully inspire others.

I taught for only three years, but one year I had a small group of extremely needy students in a class that was labeled 8+. It was for students who were still learning eighth-grade material even though many of them should have been graduated from the eighth grade years earlier. The average eighth-grader is twelve to fourteen years old. That year I had students as old as seventeen in my class. They had gotten involved in gangs or had family issues or other reasons for being truant or unsuccessful. It was a difficult group, to say the least. But I remember fondly one student named Sammy who always tried hard. I did my best to praise Sammy as much as I could in front of as many students as possible (though some days, unfortunately, that was a group as small as two students).

Though I'm not sure how many others in that 8+ class I reached, Sammy did appreciate my praise. I know this because he reached out to me on Facebook years later, thanked me for everything I had done, and told me I had inspired him to go on to finish high school and start college. That certainly felt good, and I learned a valuable lesson from it.

I only wish I had remembered that lesson on the day I publicly criticized Nicky. Unfortunately, despite my best efforts, after my public "laziness" comment, things went from bad to worse with Nicky. Someone who had been my best, most successful salesperson ended up leaving the company. Although obviously part of that was his doing, I know how wrong it was to criticize him publicly, and I will always blame myself for Nicky's undoing.

The bottom line: Praise, praise, praise, and praise some more. There is simply no downside to positive, authentic praise. If and when you feel the need to criticize, do it privately. Then go right back out and continue to praise.

FAST **F**irst **A**ction **S**teps to **T**ake:

1. Make a list of five kind, authentic things you can say about each person you manage and/or encounter on a regular basis.
2. Practice doling out praise publicly and increase the praise you give out each day. Remember, it's free and it's powerful.
3. When you do have to deliver criticism, do it privately and try doing it with a praise sandwich: praise, criticism, and then more deep praise.

11

Keeping People Happy

49. Make It a Honey Day

"Today is Honey Day," announced Brian Murray to the Likeable Media internal Facebook group. "The entire day will be dedicated to appreciating the amazing work that Honey does for us."

When I read this, I was surprised at first, but then I smiled with glee as I realized what was going on. Likeable Media had been named to the top places to work list by *Crain's* for the last three years running. Brian, our director of talent and recruitment, was looking for ways to surprise and delight the staff and decided that one way to do it would be to create a holiday just to recognize one employee—Honey—and make her feel special.

I loved many things about this. I loved how big Brian had gone; before people realized it, there were ribbons and balloons and even a cake in Honey's honor. I loved how secretive this had been; it had been a surprise not only to Honey but to the entire staff. I loved how it made Honey feel: honored, special, and excited. (I don't think she'll ever leave the company. Honestly, would you leave a company that created a holiday in your honor?)

But most of all, I loved how random the whole thing was. Don't get me wrong: From the little I know, Honey is a terrific employee. But she wasn't a manager and hadn't accomplished anything remarkable. That was the whole point, I guess. Just by recognizing someone who worked hard and represented the Likeable core values well, Brian sent a message not only to Honey but to the rest of the team, and to would-be team members, that this was a group that celebrated hard work and loved to surprise and delight.

If you've ever been to a casino, you know that one of the first things you notice as you come onto the gambling floor is the sounds of slot machines going off and people winning money. Pretty much any time day or night that you walk into a casino, you'll hear these sounds. This is not an accident. It's by design, and it's based on a powerful psychological principle called *variable rewards.* The sounds of the slot machines going off remind you that someone is winning right now, and get you thinking at some level, even if not consciously, that you could be the next winner.

When you surprise and delight your employees, your customers, your colleagues, or your family, you're using the same principle. You probably can't afford to surprise and delight everyone all the time, but by surprising and delighting some people at random and unexpected times, you get everyone thinking that she could be the recipient of that special something—whether it's a small cash bonus, a few extra vacation days, or an office holiday named in her honor—the next time.

A few months ago, my wife and I noticed that we had a rare completely free weekend and decided to surprise our daughter, Charlotte. We looked up where her favorite YouTube celebrity, Miranda Sings, was playing that weekend; found decent rates to fly from New York to Knoxville, Tennessee; and told Charlotte that thanks to her good grades and great behavior, we were rewarding her with the weekend in Knoxville. She ended up having an amazing time, even meeting Miranda. Better yet, both she and her sister Kate have been on their best behavior ever since, waiting to be rewarded with the next surprise trip.

I had the honor of meeting Charles Best, the founder and leader of one of my favorite nonprofits, DonorsChoose, which supports teachers and helps them fund classroom projects. When I asked Charles what I could do to help support them, instead of asking for a donation, he handed me a huge stack of fifty-dollar DonorsChoose gift cards. My mission was to hand out the gift cards to my influential friends, introduce them to DonorsChoose.org, and then give them the opportunity to go online and use a free gift card to support their favorite teacher. I thought I surely would be asked to give money when I offered to help but instead was surprised and delighted when I was given the "gift of giving." In turn, I was able to surprise and delight another fifty people—plus the teachers they would go online to support—and simultaneously got the word out about one of my favorite causes.

But remember, surprise and delight don't have to cost you money. It's all about making people feel special and doing things a little differently to accomplish that. Sometimes we'll start the day with a team-building activity, for instance. Other times we'll have a surprise happy hour at the end of a hard day's work. At still other times we might have a spontaneous "moment of rock" to celebrate someone's accomplishment.

But Brian Murray's Honey Day was better than anything I'd ever thought of. Over a year later, Honey is one of the most productive employees at the company, and I can't wait to find out who the next person to get his own holiday will be. Neither can the rest of the company.

FAST First Action Steps to Take:

1. Make a list of five creative ways you can surprise your employees, colleagues, clients, or family.
2. Experiment with creative ways to offer those surprises, and delight your people either directly because of something awesome they've done or, better yet, "just because."
3. Try to surprise and delight people every day, even in little ways: Praise, kind words, and the little things often go as far as the big things.

50. Go Back in Time and Write a Thank You Card (Yes, a Real One)

"Wow!" I exclaimed with excitement. I was staring at a thank you card I had received from the CEO of a multibillion-dollar company. I had interviewed Sheldon Yellen, the CEO of the property-restoration company BELFOR, for a previous book, and just a few days later I had gotten the thank you card in the mail.

Truthfully, the thank you card was barely legible (I think Sheldon has about as good handwriting as I have), but it felt incredible nonetheless. The guy was running a huge company, had a family of his own, and had just starred on the CBS television show *Undercover Boss,* yet he had taken some very precious time out of his day to write a thank you card to me, someone he had never met.

I thought about that card for a while. I thought about the last time *I* had written thank you cards. It was probably after my wedding nine years earlier! A lot had happened in those nine years. Email had continued to become more and more widespread. Cell phone plans had changed, and now everyone I knew had unlimited text messages. Facebook hadn't opened up beyond college students at the time of my wedding, and Twitter didn't exist.

With all the major technological advancements of the last nine years, I realized there were now easier and easier ways to say thank you. You could say thanks with a text, tweet, email, or private message on Facebook or LinkedIn. But I wondered whether a handwritten thank you card would be better received.

I thought about how I felt getting that thank you card from Sheldon Yellen and imagined how I'd have felt if it instead had been a thank you email or text message. It would have felt very different and not nearly as special.

Since I was in the middle of doing research for my book *Likeable Business*, I decided to ask a few CEOs I was planning to interview already what their experience with giving and receiving thank you cards was. As it turned out, most of the CEOs I talked to said that when they received handwritten thank you cards, they were much more likely to read them than they were when they received emails. I found it fascinating that some of the most successful, busiest people in the world would stop and read a handwritten note sooner than they'd read an email or tweet.

Even more interesting was how many of the people I talked to believed in *sending* handwritten cards. Besides Sheldon, there was the CEO of Restaurant.com, Cary Chessick; the happiness guru Shawn Achor; and the business leader and Columbia professor Srikumar Rao. All were avid fans of the handwritten thank you note. Most notably, there was Charles Best, whom I interviewed.

Charles Best is the founder and CEO of DonorsChoose, the online nonprofit organization that I mentioned in Chapter 49.

Charles shared with me the results of a study he had conducted to demonstrate the return on investment of gratitude. In that experiment, the DonorsChoose staff sent handwritten thank you notes to half of their recent first-time donors. The other half did not receive thank you notes. The results showed a direct correlation between being thanked by card and the likelihood of giving again. In fact, those who were personally thanked were 38 percent more likely to give another donation, proving an actual ROI of gratitude. Plus, when they gave, they gave more on average.

Though I thought I had been practicing gratitude in our business and in my life by regularly thanking staff and customers by email, an email thank you is just not that special these days. Emails are supereasy to write and send, and although some people may appreciate receiving them, others may resent you for cluttering their in-boxes.

I vowed to begin to write personalized thank you notes. I knew it would be hard to stick to something like this, so I began by writing one card per week on Wednesday and then increased it to three personalized thank you notes each Wednesday. Finally, I increased the quota to three thank you notes each weekday, which I usually would write on the train to work.

The experiment proved powerful very quickly. Some recipients of my notes said they were moved to tears, and others replied by sending nice tweets. But it was clear that everyone appreciated the extra time it took to handwrite a thank you card, seal it, and deliver or send it. In an increasingly digital world, there was something magical about receiving a handwritten note.

My hope and expectation is that thank you cards will help you build loyalty, pride, and, yes, influence among your team members and with your customers, partners, friends, and family. But no matter what, it still feels darn good to write and send them. The amazing thing about gratefulness and unselfishness is this: Whether or not there's an immediate return on investment in terms of business value, there's always an immediate result in terms of your happiness.

You will literally feel your mood elevate as you write each thank you card. As we talked about before, that will help put you in a good position to keep the people around you happy. Thus, thank you cards really work doubly to inspire, motivate, and keep the people around you happy.

I know it's very old-fashioned to advocate for thank you cards as much as I do. But the very fact that it is so old-fashioned and even out of fashion is what makes writing and sending the cards so special. Today, I still begin each day by writing out three or four thank you cards to staff, customers, partners, friends, and family. It's an essential part of my day and has helped make me a much better leader and human being. And for that, to Sheldon Yellen, Charles Best, and the others who have inspired me, I say, "Thank you!"

FAST First Action Steps to Take:

1. Buy a pack of thank you cards at the local drugstore or stationery store; you can even order personalized ones online. Do it without delay.
2. Write one thank you card the next morning you have an opportunity. Do it as early in the day as you can and hand-deliver it as quickly as possible. The faster the feedback comes, the more inspired you'll be to keep going.
3. Practice doing this every day until it becomes a habit. Only you know how quickly and profoundly you can make this process habitual, but you will feel happier along the way no matter what.

51. An Intro a Day Goes a Long Way

9/21/13

Dave and Bob, you remind me of each other, so I thought it was about time you met. You're both bestselling authors, go-givers, entrepreneurs, and immensely likeable guys.

Happy connecting, and shana tova to both of you!
Adam

Adam M. Grant, Ph.D.
Wharton professor and author of *Give and Take*
www.giveandtake.com

When I received this email in my in-box in September 2013, I was a little surprised. I barely knew the sender, Adam Grant; we'd had one prior conversation, but that was it. I hadn't asked for an introduction and hadn't done anything to indicate to Adam that I wanted or needed an introduction to Bob.

As it turned out, though, Adam was right. Bob and I did have a lot in common, and there could be opportunities to collaborate. At the least, it was clear that it might be superhelpful for me to connect with a successful author and speaker such as Bob, whom I definitely had heard of before the intro. I thanked Adam and emailed Bob to connect and then went on with my day.

A few weeks later, I got another email introduction from Adam. At that point I was shocked. Again, I had had one phone conversation with the man but had never met him, helped him, or asked him for anything. I had to figure out what was going on, and so I decided to read Grant's book, *Give and Take.*

That book is one of the best books I've ever read. With both great stories and tons of research-based data, Grant makes a powerful argument that in business and in life, givers win. *Give and Take* also introduced me to another Adam, Adam Rifkin.

Adam Rifkin makes three introductions a day. His introductions have led to two marriages, hundreds of jobs, dozens of companies being funded, and at least twelve new business partnerships.

Contrary to what you might think, Rifkin is not a typical people person. In fact, he is a shy introvert who as a successful serial tech entrepreneur doesn't have a lot of time to network. Yet as Adam told my friend Michael Simmons in an interview for *Forbes,* "If you already have a network, an introduction is the most powerful daily action you can take to build it. In just a few minutes, you can have a dramatic impact on the lives of two people and generate a large amount of goodwill for yourself and the overall community you're building."

At its heart, an introduction does two things. First, it endorses the two people you're introducing. It tells each of them that the other is worth connecting with. Second, it provides information on why the two people should connect.

If you've done an intro well, both parties can benefit. Better yet, you, too, will benefit, as both parties will appreciate you for having thought of them and connecting them. Best yet, it doesn't take long to make an introduction. This powerful tool is described by Grant as a "five-minute favor."

It's nice to make an intro when one party asks you for one, of course, but it's even more meaningful when you can make a totally unsolicited intro, as Grant did for Bob Berg and me. Think about the people in your network, especially the ones you haven't spoken with in a while. Think about who might mutually benefit from connecting. Then use LinkedIn or email to make a simple introduction. The one at the start of this chapter is a perfect example. In a concise yet compelling note, tell each person who the other person is. (Better yet, rave about each person to the other.) Then suggest that they connect and hint at why it might be mutually beneficial. This second part is especially important if you're introducing busy people who may not have a lot of spare time to meet someone new. (Doesn't that describe us all, though?)

As with writing thank you cards, the hard part is making a system of this practice. Using social media, Rifkin has managed to do just that, as the *Forbes* article continued: "Adam has marked 50 people as 'close friends' on Facebook and set up notifications on Twitter for people he wants to build a deeper relationship with. What this means is that he is more likely to see all of these people's updates," which often provides him with a specific reason to reach out to someone (e.g., "I saw that Dave is working on a new book about the art of people. Since Adam is such a master of people skills, I thought you might have some things to talk about").

"Before these tools existed, you would have to ask people, 'What's new?' Now, you don't have to do small talk to see where they are. The social networks push it to you."

He then thinks of relevant, potentially useful introductions for the people in his network and turns to LinkedIn to make them. Since Rifkin joined LinkedIn in December 2003, he has consistently made three introductions per day. That means he has made a mind-boggling ten thousand introductions.

Introductions keep you top of mind with the important people in your network and can have a life-changing impact on the individuals you introduce. And you can do it all in just a few minutes a day.

I'm finally getting together with Bob Berg, the man Adam Grant kindly introduced me to two years ago. I can't wait to find out what happens next.

FAST First Action Steps to Take:

1. Take an inventory of your network, beginning with LinkedIn and going on to social networks, email, the contacts in your phone, and perhaps even an old-fashioned Rolodex. Write down the names of thirty people you haven't talked to in a while.
2. Match up each of the thirty names with other people in your network who might mutually benefit from an introduction. Write down these thirty names next to your first thirty.
3. Begin introducing the people in the network whose names you have written down. Start with just one per day no matter how excited you are, so that you don't burn out too quickly and are more likely to build up endurance in this new exercise. Practice until you develop a habit of making introductions.

52. Buy Him a Bonsai

What the heck can we get a man who has everything?" I asked my chief of staff, Meg. We had just had our first successful meeting with Rich, a venture capitalist in New York, and were trying to think of something nice to send as a thank-you for meeting with us. This was my first time raising money from institutional investors, and I was feeling pretty intimidated by the whole process.

These VCs typically were pitched by at least a hundred people per month. That's over five pushy entrepreneurs per workday. They were used to saying no to just about everyone who pitched them.

I had begun my practice of handwritten thank you cards by then, but I felt that wouldn't be enough. Also, at the meeting, I had given him one of my books. I wanted to send something special, something memorable. But like most VCs, this guy Rich was, well, rich. By all accounts, he really had everything he ever needed in terms of material wealth. Well, maybe not a yacht, but since I couldn't send him that, I was struggling with what kind of thank you gift to send as a follow-up.

"What about a bonsai?" Meg asked totally out of the blue. "A bonsai is special, easy to grow, and lasts a long time."

As soon as she said that, I knew we had it. A bonsai would be the perfect gift for the venture capitalist who had everything. I asked Meg to look into ordering a bonsai (as we'd obviously never done that before) and began to write out the note that would accompany it:

Dear Rich,

Here's to your growth, our growth, and the growth of this bonsai. Enjoy.

Best,
Dave Kerpen

I was so excited! A bonsai would be so easy to take care of and would grow for years, just like an investment in our company, Likeable Local. We ordered the bonsai and sent it with my note for two-day delivery and waited with anticipation for Rich to receive it.

Unfortunately, we got a response from Rich before he had received the bonsai. Rich had chosen to pass on investing in Likeable Local. He said by email that he "liked the business a lot. But I'm just not so sure whether it will scale."

I was devastated. Honestly, of course, I was upset about getting rejected by a VC, but after having worked so hard to find the perfect thank you gift for someone who didn't need anything, I was even more upset that I had been rejected before the gift arrived.

Luckily, Meg, my supertalented chief of staff who's always there for me, was there again.

"Dave, first of all, I'm sure he'll reply again after he gets the bonsai. Second of all, you never know what the future will bring," she said. "And third, perhaps most important, no matter what happens here, I think we're onto something!"

Meg was right.

The next day, Rich replied again with a thank-you for the bonsai. He wrote: "Thanks much for the thoughtful bonsai, Dave! I love it. Let's hope I can take better care of it than I did for your company."

Considering that Rich had just rejected me, his joke wasn't very reassuring. However, I received another email the next day: "Hey Dave. I want to introduce you to Tim, a fellow VC who's more bullish on SMB-focused businesses than I am. Tim, Dave is a great, thoughtful entrepreneur. You two should definitely connect."

The point is that for those people you want to keep happy and influence positively, it is generally worth it to purchase and send a thoughtful gift. A bonsai is the perfect gift for venture capitalists and other investors because it grows, as they want their investments to do, and because it's thoughtful and even classy without being too expensive. (We buy them now in bulk for about $35 each.) If wealthy venture capitalists appreciate a $35 bonsai, surely so will anyone else in your life.

Of course, most people will appreciate any type of thoughtful gift; it doesn't have to be a bonsai. In addition to bonsais, books, and thank you cards, we've sent trophies, bottles of wine, mini herb gardens, chocolates, and lots of giant foam thumbs. We even sent a toy moat to one investor who said we needed to build a better moat to protect our business before he'd invest.

They say it's the thought that counts, but to me, when it comes to giving memorable thank-yous, it's both the thought and the execution that count. It's all about thinking outside the box and sending something that nobody else would send and that will make the recipient smile.

As for the connection Rich made to Tim? It took a while, but Tim eventually wrote me a nice check to invest in our company. He got a really nice bonsai the next day.

FAST **F**irst **A**ction **S**teps to **T**ake:

1. Write down the names of five important people in your career and/or life whom you'd really like to keep happy.
2. For each of those five people, brainstorm a thoughtful, affordable thank you gift that nobody else would send and that will make the recipient smile. (It's okay to go with a bonsai if you can't think of anything else.)
3. Start a thank you gift closet. Purchase a stockpile of creative thank you gifts and then send them out regularly, not on special occasions, ideally with handwritten notes.

When it comes to **giving memorable thank-yous**, it's all about thinking **outside of the box** and sending something that **nobody else** would send and that will make the **recipient smile**.

53. Be Unoriginal, Part 2: How to Remain Top of Mind for Thousands of People Every Day

"If you build it, they won't come, Dave."

Those words, spoken by my wife and business partner, Carrie, stuck like a knife in me. For one thing, my favorite movie was *Field of Dreams*, and so when she riffed off of its most famous line in a negative way, it wasn't easy to listen to.

Another reason it stung is that I realized that as usual, Carrie was right. It was 2008, and we were talking about the new social media–driven Web that was quickly emerging at that time. What Carrie was so poetically saying was that the days of building a website and then expecting people to surf the Web and simply find it were quickly ending. In fact, fewer and fewer people were even using the expression "surf the Web." Instead, it seemed, the Web was surfing people through the reliable waves that were Facebook, Twitter, and LinkedIn.

Fortunately, I agreed with Carrie. We brainstormed what to do about this problem and realized that instead of building beautiful websites and destinations for companies, we could build beautiful and valuable content and then help companies get people's attention by distributing it where people were spending their time: on the social networks.

"If we build it, we can come to them," we reasoned. The strategy worked, and we were able to base two successful companies on this notion.

During that process, we began working on our personal brands as well. We realized that if social media could help grow brands and small businesses, we could do the same thing for ourselves. The field of personal branding has exploded in the last few years, and today many people see the value of using social media to get a better job, find new customers or partners, or land a better book deal, to name a few outcomes.

But back in 2008 we felt like pioneers. The strategy was the same one we used for our businesses: Build it and then come to people. In other words, build social media accounts and then create, curate, and share great, valuable content on a regular basis. When I lived in Boston, my favorite sports radio station was WEEI. I took those letters and applied them to content across social media: Entertain people. Educate people. Inspire people (EEI).

The strategy worked, and we each gained many thousands of followers across Facebook, Twitter, and LinkedIn. One thing was for sure: We helped demonstrate that good content alone can rise to the top. At one point, I had more page views (20 million–plus) on LinkedIn than Bill Gates, Jack Welch, and Mark Cuban combined. It certainly wasn't because of intelligence, wealth, or success; it was because I shared more and arguably better content than those guys did.

But it has gotten noisier and noisier in social media as more and more brands, small businesses, and individuals have begun to create more and more content in an effort to come to consumers. The result is what my author friend Mark Schaefer calls "content shock." There's just too much content and not enough time for people to get through it all.

The good news is that instead of having to become a content factory, constantly churning out endless amounts of entertaining, educational, and inspiring content to feed the beast of social media, you can become a great curator. The content is already out there; all you have to do is find the EEI content that best resonates with you and that you think will resonate with your own network, and be the one who shares it.

I'm going to let you in on a little secret about social media: Few people pay attention to who created great content, but everyone remembers whom they got it from. Of course, you should always quote the sources of your content. Also, there's nothing wrong with creating your own original blog posts, tweets, and LinkedIn updates; it's just very time-consuming.

It is much easier to be the best curator, to find great sources and queue up most of your content in advance. The social networks you should be doing this for depend on your goals, but for most people, LinkedIn and Twitter are great places to start. (Facebook is good, too, but is more personal and private than the other two.) There are lots of free tools available to help you curate and schedule great content (Likeable Hub from our company is one such free tool).

By scheduling lots of great content for social media, you'll end up literally at the top of people's news feeds and therefore at the top of their minds. Just about every day someone in my network says something to the effect of "I see you everywhere! Love your content, keep it up." Meanwhile, a lot of "my" content is actually other people's: valuable educational articles and how-to guides I find, entertaining videos and infographics I find, and inspirational quotes and stories I find. EEI. Not my own, but carefully curated to my audiences.

The best part about social media is how well it scales. One good article can be shared, seen, and appreciated by hundreds or even thousands of people. Think about the old days and how great salespeople and small-business owners stayed top of mind through written and mailed letters or newspaper or radio ads. Now the same letter that used to reach a single person can reach thousands or tens of thousands or even millions without any more cost or effort.

Of course, you also can use technological tools to reach people privately and stay top of mind in a more personal, intimate way. Whereas LinkedIn and Twitter are great tools for mass branding, Snapchat, WhatsApp, and texting are excellent tools for building relationships one at a time. Sometimes people appreciate getting an article, tip, idea, or quote directly from you in a private forum rather than seeing it as a public share with the world. If you meet someone important you want to influence, get her contact info and without being pushy and never asking for anything send her a private message sharing content you think she'll find particularly valuable.

I tweeted at *Shark Tank* star and serial entrepreneur and investor Lori Greiner about a year ago one night when I saw her promoting her book during an episode of the show. But instead of a public tweet I sent her a direct, private message saying I'd be happy to help her promote her book. I was surprised and excited when she replied with her cell phone number.

Within a week and before we even had a phone call, Lori and I were texting each other furiously, and contrary to the popular belief that electronic communication lacks intimacy, we were building up way more intimate a relationship than we could have done with a call or perhaps even with a meeting. I texted her several articles on how to launch a bestselling book, only one of which I had written, and she appreciated it. She ended up with an Amazon bestseller a few weeks later, and I ended up with a new friend. A year later, Lori was there for me when I needed a favor or two. And we've still never met face-to-face!

Keeping people happy is not an easy task. Keeping a large following happy is even harder. However, you don't have to be an original-content machine to be top of mind for people while building your personal brand. You just have to know where to find that content and how to become the best curator in your network.

FAST **F**irst **A**ction **S**teps to **T**ake:

1. If you're not already on LinkedIn or Twitter, join one of those key social networks for building your personal brand. If you're already on one network, join the other.

2. Spend thirty minutes looking for educational, entertaining, and inspiring (EEI) content. Keep a master list and begin to share and schedule the content for your social networks.
3. Find content appropriate for five key individuals in your network and send it to them privately through Snapchat or WhatsApp or in a text message.
4. Make a habit of finding and sharing EEI content on a regular basis. At a minimum, you can do this by scheduling thirty minutes a week for the process of curation.

Conclusion

Getting Everything You Want in Life Is All About People and the Ultimate Paradox

I've gotten some really great advice from some terrific people over the years. I've been fortunate to meet world-class business leaders, authors, and mentors. But probably the most compelling piece of advice I've ever heard was from my wife, Carrie, who turned to me one day while we were sitting on the couch. The moment couldn't have been more random; it was just a normal Saturday afternoon on a cool, crisp autumn day. The kids were upstairs playing, and neither of us was talking business. We had just finished lunch, and we were having a rare totally relaxing moment on the couch, when Carrie turned to me and said:

"You know, the ultimate paradox is that the secret to getting everything you want at work and in life is treating people well, not trying to get everything you want. Meet the right people, listen well, connect and inspire them, and they'll want to give you everything that you want. They'll want to do this so badly, you won't even need to ask!"

"You're a genius," I replied. And she was dead right.

The days of forcing or bullying your way to the top are over. The loudest, most aggressive, most assertive people are no longer the winners in business and in life. The needy, whiny, pushy people might have been successful in the past and might even be successful in the short term today, but they won't be the winners in the future. Instead, the winners will be the people who know how to understand themselves and connect with and work well with others.

We've spent a lot of time together talking about how to understand yourself and others better, how to listen better, how to connect on a deeper level, and how to influence people. We've also discussed the conflicts and challenges that may emerge.

We've talked about how to teach people, inspire people, and keep the people around you happy at work, at home, and in your entire network.

Although these methods won't lead to instant success, they will position you to be the person whom people want to be around, the person whom people know, like, and trust—and yes, the person people *want to help succeed.*

Follow *The Art of People* playbook and people will want to help you get everything you want at work and in life.

This may be the end of the book, but it's the beginning of our journey together. As I urged you in the Introduction, I will urge you again: Connect with me as early and as much as you'd like. I want more than anything to help you succeed in mastering the people skills you've learned in these pages. So tweet me, LinkedIn with me, email me if you'd like. You can even schedule a free one-to-one video chat with me at ScheduleDave.com. I'm looking forward to seeing you grow and succeed.

The *Art of People* is just that—it's an art and not always a science. But if you've read this far and especially if you've done the FAST action steps at the end of every chapter, you've already begun to master the art of people. Here's to your continued success!

Acknowledgments

So much went into getting this book in front of you, and I am deeply grateful to the people who made it possible, both the ones named below and the many people who support me whose names aren't below.

First and foremost, to my wife, Carrie, you have taught me more about the art of people than anyone, and I appreciate you more than you'll ever know. Thank you for joining me in the journey of life. To my children, Charlotte, Kate, and Seth, thank you for putting up with Daddy while I was writing this book, and I promise, the children's book you keep asking me about is still to come. To our nanny, Joyce, thank you for making life so much easier for Carrie and my family while I worked on this book and ran a company at the same time.

Thanks to Mom, Dad, Phil, Dan, Danny, Da, Mimi, Mark and Lisa, and the rest of my family for all of your unconditional love and support.

To my chief of staff, Meg Riedinger, my number two in so many ways, thank you for all you have done and continue to do to make me more productive, more efficient, and happier. I am so blessed to have you in my life. To my CTO, Hugh Morgenbesser; my VP of Marketing, Nicole Kroese; my VP of Sales, Mark Brooks; and the rest of our awesome team at Likeable Local, thank you for running the ship while I was out writing. You are the best team ever.

To Candie Harris, Rachel Hadley, and the team at Likeable Media, thank you for your brave leadership. Thanks as well to all of our Likeable advisors: Milind Mehere, Mark Roberge, Peg Jackson, Craig

Gibson, Ed Zuckerberg, and Nihal Mehta. And thanks to our investors: Dave McClure, Thomas Dibenedetto, Don Douglas, Mark Shufro, Ben Rosner, Verne Harnish, Creel Price, Daniel Fisher, Jean and John Dziewit, Maurice Reznik, Erik Qualman, Roy Rodenstein, Armando Biondi, Brent Beshore, Brian Jacob, Brian Savage, David Chie, Jed Breed, Jimmy Vosika, Lance McCollough, Navneet Aron, Todd Geismann, Tom Meusel, Travis Huff, Barbara Morgenbesser, and Trevor Folsom.

To my friends, thank you for inspiring me and being there for me. My EO Forum Mates are truly people I can call up at 3 A.M. to talk to about anything. Thank you Ben Rosner, Andy Cohen, Jeff Bernstein, Vincent Cannariato, Kevin Gilbert, Ryan Payne, and Dana Haddad. To my world tour friends, thanks for always providing laughs and opportunities to play PtP: Steve Evangelista, Kevin Anannab, Tad Bruneau, Andy Kaufmann, Matt Sichel, Sean Fleischman, and Kevin Aeschelman. To my BU friends, thank you for being fabulous: Marvin Dunson III, Meg Simione, Rishi Lulla, Sarah Bestrout, Danika Whitehouse, Chad Flahive, Aaron Kaburick, David Pimentel, Alyssa Malaspina, and Hilary Wall. To my Port Washington friends, thank you for being the most neighborly people around: Jamie Packer, Ken Ruskin, Jeremy Rochester, Scott Baxter, and David Heydt.

To my publishing family, thanks for making this dream into a reality. Celeste Fine, you are the best agent on the planet. John Maas, you are a fabulous new addition to the team. Talia Krohn, thank you for shepherding this idea—I owe you a bonsai or two. To Wade Lucas, thank you for taking my words and helping me deliver them to more people around the world. To the rest of the team at Crown, thank you for all you have done to make my words come alive.

To all of my Influencer and author friends online and offline, thank you for inspiring me with your words and even more so with your actions.

To everyone who's crossed paths with me, and to all who have helped to shape me and these words, I say, THANK YOU.

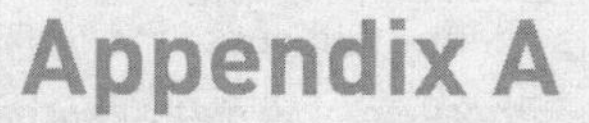

Appendix A

Enneagram Assessment

This assessment originally appeared in *Awareness to Action: The Enneagram, Emotional Intelligence, and Change* by Robert Tallon and Mario Sikora. I have made a few minor changes to adapt it to this book. For more information about the Enneagram, visit www.enneagramlearning.com.

PERSONALITY TYPE A

Score the statements according to how true or applicable they are to you.

1	2	3	4	5
Almost Never	**Rarely**	**Sometimes**	**Frequently**	**Almost Always**

___ Creative and have an artistic view of life.

___ Feel different from others, as if "on the outside looking in."

___ Tend to experience more melancholy than most people I know.

___ Tend to be overly sensitive.

___ Feel that something is missing in my life.

___ Feel envious of other people's relationships, lifestyles, and accomplishments.

___ Thrive in environments where I can express my creativity.

___ When misunderstood, can become withdrawn, self-conscious, and/or rebellious.

___ Tend to be romantic and long for the great love of my life to come along.
___ Can be caught in a fantasy world of romance and imagination.
___ Enjoy having elegant, refined, unique things that no one else has.
___ Attracted to what is intense and out of the ordinary.
___ Tend to be moody, withdrawn, and self-absorbed when stressed.
___ Tend to be compassionate, expressive, and supportive when not stressed.
___ Can be deeply hurt by the slightest criticism.
___ Tend to be reflective and to search for the meaning of my life.
___ Strive to be unique and have done things to avoid being ordinary.
___ Manners and good taste are extremely important to me.
___ People have seen me as overly dramatic.
___ Believe it is important to understand my own and other people's feelings.

Total Score______

PERSONALITY TYPE B

Score the statements according to how true or applicable they are to you.

1	2	3	4	5
Almost Never	**Rarely**	**Sometimes**	**Frequently**	**Almost Always**

___ Have a strong sense of responsibility and am a hard worker.
___ Try to prepare for every contingency.
___ Suspicious of others and wonder about their motives.
___ Making decisions on my own may cause me anxiety.
___ Safety and security are priorities in my life.
___ Doubt my own decisions and opinions about myself.
___ Believe it is important for people to be with other people or to belong to a group or an organization.
___ Value the belief that everything is going to be all right yet often lack faith in this belief.

___ Friends and family provide the support I feel is necessary in life.
___ Tend to take things too seriously and overreact to small issues.
___ Don't really trust anybody I haven't known for a long time.
___ Look for danger, unsafe people, or unsafe situations.
___ Tend to be suspicious, anxious, and defensive when stressed.
___ Tend to be caring, warm, and loyal when not stressed.
___ When feeling anxious I can be overly vigilant and controlling.
___ When feeling relaxed I tend to be friendly and responsive to people.
___ In a relationship, it has been difficult for me to trust the commitment of the other person.
___ When afraid of something, I've done what was necessary to overcome my fear.
___ Tend to worry more than other people.
___ Motivated by the need to acquire security and social support.

Total Score______

PERSONALITY TYPE C

Score the statements according to how true or applicable they are to you.

1	2	3	4	5
Almost Never	**Rarely**	**Sometimes**	**Frequently**	**Almost Always**

___ Dislike confrontation and try to keep the peace.
___ Easygoing, "laid back," and optimistic.
___ Listen patiently and can be very understanding and comforting to friends.
___ Tend to procrastinate and ignore problems or brush them under the rug.
___ Attracted to habits and routines, can relax easily and tune out reality through TV, daydreaming, a good book, etc.
___ Have difficulty making decisions because "everything looks good."
___ Routine and structure help me stay focused and accomplish things.

___ Can be forgetful, neglectful, and "fuzzy" about details.

___ Can feel angry even though I might look peaceful.

___ Get tired easily and would love to take time during the day to relax and renew my energy.

___ Can be a "homebody" and enjoy the comfort and peace of home.

___ In relationships, I seek harmony and peace through a sense of belonging and/or by bonding with the other person.

___ Dislike people nagging me; this makes me quite stubborn.

___ May do routine and unimportant things before I tackle an important job.

___ Tend to be withdrawn, forgetful, stubborn, and passive-aggressive when stressed.

___ Tend to be open-minded, receptive, and very patient when not stressed.

___ Tend to go along with what people say just to get them off my back.

___ Too much to do or too many decisions to make can make me angry, anxious, and/or depressed.

___ Am told I'm a "nice guy" and dislike putting myself first.

___ Motivated by the need to maintain peace of mind and harmony in my life.

Total Score______

PERSONALITY TYPE D

Score the statements according to how true or applicable they are to you.

1	2	3	4	5
Almost Never	**Rarely**	**Sometimes**	**Frequently**	**Almost Always**

___ Tend to be more emotional than most people I know.

___ Consider relationships the most important part of my life.

___ See myself as caring and helpful and like to make people feel special and loved.

___ Have trouble saying no to requests.

___ Giving feels more comfortable than receiving.

___ Need to feel close to people and feel rejected and hurt if I don't experience that closeness.
___ Like feeling indispensable and helping others become successful.
___ Like to be gracious, outgoing, and connected with people.
___ Avoid expressing negative feelings and like to compliment and flatter people.
___ Have a strong need to be noticed, liked, and appreciated for what I do for others.
___ Like people to depend on me and deliver on my promises.
___ In intimate relationships, I value being told that I'm loved and wanted.
___ People feel comfortable telling me their problems.
___ Work very hard at maintaining relationships.
___ Tend to be possessive and demanding when stressed.
___ Tend to be loving, caring, and supportive when not stressed.
___ Know how to get people to like me.
___ Can act like a martyr when not appreciated.
___ Believe that my motives for helping others are noble and helpful.
___ Motivated by the need to be appreciated, loved, and connected to people.

Total Score______

PERSONALITY TYPE E

Score the statements according to how true or applicable they are to you.

1	2	3	4	5
Almost Never	**Rarely**	**Sometimes**	**Frequently**	**Almost Always**

___ Good at marketing and selling myself and my ideas.
___ Like doing more than one or two things at a time; enjoy "multitasking."
___ Want to be "number one" and am confident in my abilities.
___ Love to work and be productive, and work has tended to be a top priority in my life.

___ Have been goal-oriented for as long as I can remember.

___ Value looking good, presenting a good first impression, and "dressing for success."

___ Getting a product to market before the competition is more important than holding it back until it is "perfect."

___ Prefer being with people to being alone.

___ Value finding the most practical, effective way to do a job.

___ To impress, I may take on too much and make promises I can't keep.

___ Have been told I am not in touch with my emotions.

___ Believe that competition is a good thing and tend to be very competitive.

___ Value exceeding standards and rising to the top of my profession.

___ Tend to "spin" the facts and be overly self-promoting when stressed.

___ Tend to be honest, competent, and charming when not stressed.

___ Believe that negative feelings are an obstacle to getting the job done.

___ Find it easy to adapt to different people and situations.

___ Enjoy supporting the careers of people whom I care about and who deserve it.

___ Have difficulty understanding why people settle for second best.

___ Motivated by being outstanding and being recognized for my personal success and achievements.

Total Score_____

PERSONALITY TYPE F

Score the statements according to how true or applicable they are to you.

1	2	3	4	5
Almost Never	**Rarely**	**Sometimes**	**Frequently**	**Almost Always**

___ Uncomfortable around loud, emotional people.

___ Enjoy analyzing things, gathering data, and figuring out what makes things tick.

___ Tend to be shy and withdrawn, especially at social events.
___ Tend to be more comfortable expressing ideas than emotions, especially spontaneously.
___ May hesitate while I try to organize my thoughts and may not speak at all if I'm not comfortable with what I want to say.
___ Try to avoid confrontations.
___ Enjoy spending time alone pursuing my personal interests.
___ Sensitive to criticism but try to hide that sensitivity.
___ Enjoy the sense of independence that comes from living frugally.
___ Prefer people not to know how I feel or what I think unless I tell them.
___ People may find it difficult to follow my train of thought.
___ Enjoy having control of my own time and private space.
___ Easily annoyed by people who act unintelligent or uninformed.
___ Have ideas, theories, and opinions about almost everything.
___ Tend to socialize with people who are interested in the same things I am.
___ Tend to be distant, stubborn, and pessimistic when stressed.
___ Tend to be insightful, objective, and sensitive when not stressed.
___ Can be critical, cynical, and argumentative and can act intellectually superior.
___ Don't mind working alone and enjoy being self-sufficient.
___ Rely on facts rather than emotions to make decisions.

Total Score______

PERSONALITY TYPE G

Score the statements according to how true or applicable they are to you.

1	2	3	4	5
Almost Never	**Rarely**	**Sometimes**	**Frequently**	**Almost Always**

___ Feel that life is to be enjoyed and am optimistic about the future.
___ Talkative, playful, and at times uninhibited.

___ Like to leave my options open; "don't hem me in" describes me well.

___ Have lots of friends and acquaintances and support them by cheering them up.

___ Need to feel stimulated and like new, fun, exciting, and different things.

___ Tend to be idealistic and ambitious and want to contribute something positive to the world.

___ Like to entertain and enjoy telling stories and getting laughs.

___ Like to be "on the go" and may appear hyperactive to people.

___ Enjoy trying many things and can do many different things fairly well.

___ Hate to be bored and avoid doing boring, mundane things.

___ Tend to do things in excess and to always want more.

___ I'm supersensitive to possessive people; they make me feel uncomfortable.

___ Have acted inappropriately, undisciplined, and/or rebellious when stressed.

___ Tend to be fun-loving, imaginative, and optimistic when not stressed.

___ When I find work that I like, I can be very productive and enthusiastic.

___ See no value in enduring suffering and pain and try to avoid it.

___ Become frustrated if there is not enough time to do all the fun things I want to do.

___ Dislike being around pessimistic, negative people.

___ Tend to be excited and impatient about accomplishing plans.

___ Motivated to feel excited, satisfied, and happy and to do and experience more.

Total Score______

PERSONALITY TYPE H

Score the statements according to how true or applicable they are to you.

1	2	3	4	5
Almost Never	**Rarely**	**Sometimes**	**Frequently**	**Almost Always**

___ Stand up for what I want and need in life.

___ People see me as courageous and look to me as a natural leader.

___ Value strength and autonomy, take pride in taking care of my own needs, and expect others to do the same for themselves.

___ Impatient with people who are indirect or indecisive.

___ Am assertive and like to compete and win.

___ Am extremely protective of my loved ones and feel good about helping the underdog.

___ Like expressing my power and being the boss and/or being in charge.

___ I am not gullible; you must earn my trust, and I will challenge your loyalty.

___ Like taking risks and the excitement of competition.

___ Work hard and know how to get things done.

___ Love to be challenged and enjoy a good fight.

___ Would rather be respected than liked.

___ Feel I must take charge because I am the strongest and most decisive person in the group.

___ Proud about being direct, telling it "like it is," and expressing "tough love."

___ Tend to be rebellious, controlling, and insensitive when stressed.

___ Tend to be energetic, self-confident, and helpful when not stressed.

___ Am uncomfortable expressing emotions other than anger.

___ When I trust people, I can let down my guard and be more sensitive.

___ Tend to go overboard in the pursuit of fun and pleasure.

___ Motivated by the need to protect myself and my loved ones and to be powerful and in control of my life.

Total Score______

PERSONALITY TYPE I

Score the statements according to how true or applicable they are to you.

1	2	3	4	5
Almost Never	**Rarely**	**Sometimes**	**Frequently**	**Almost Always**

___ Have a strong sense of right and wrong and strive for perfection.

___ Take pride in being self-disciplined, moderate, and fair.

___ Personal integrity is extremely important to me.

___ Tend to be more logical than emotional.

___ Can be too serious and lack spontaneity.

___ Critical of myself (my own worst critic) and find it easy to be judgmental and critical of other people as well.

___ Easily discern what is wrong in a situation and how it could be done better.

___ Tend to be a workaholic and a perfectionist.

___ Value being well organized and punctual in myself and others.

___ Morals and ethics are more important than compassion and tolerance.

___ Tend to see the glass as "half empty" and to look for what needs fixing.

___ Do not consider being a perfectionist a negative thing and like to make sure all the details are just right.

___ Tend to be intolerant, inflexible, and demanding when stressed.

___ Tend to be rational, reasonable, and accepting when not stressed.

___ Fear being criticized or judged as being improper by other people.

___ Find it difficult to forgive and can carry a grudge for a long time.

___ Have difficulty seeing the "gray" areas of an issue and tend to see things in black and white.
___ Have difficulty admitting I'm wrong.
___ Believe that rules, regulations, policies, and procedures have a purpose and should be followed and am frustrated when others break rules.
___ Motivated by the need to be correct, fair, and self-disciplined.

Total Score______

IDENTIFYING YOUR PERSONALITY TYPE

Scoring Instructions

1. Transfer your scores from the Total Scores line at the bottom of each section to the appropriate lines below. For example, the score from *Personality Type A* should be recorded on the line directly below A. The numbers beneath the lines on this page correspond to the Enneagram personality types. Your highest score usually, but not always, indicates your type.

A	B	C	D	E	F	G	H	I
Score								
___	___	___	___	___	___	___	___	___
Corresponding Type								
4	6	9	2	3	5	7	8	1

2. Enter your three highest scores and their corresponding types in the appropriate boxes below.

First Highest Type		Second Highest Type		Third Highest Type	

3. Record the type from question 2 above (4, 6, 9, 2, 3, 5, 7, 8, or 1) associated with your First Highest Type.

4. Now read the "Descriptions of the Types" beginning on the next page. Which type description best fits you?

5. If questions 3 and 4 do not agree, what is your best estimation of your personality type?

Descriptions of the Types

Ones: Ones interact with the world by Striving to Be Perfect. They are often models of decorum, clear logic, and appropriate behavior. They focus on rules, procedures, and making sure that they are always doing the "right thing." When they overdo their Striving to Be Perfect, they can become critical, judgmental, and unwilling to take risks. Under stress, Ones may fear that if they have too much fun, they will become irresponsible.
Pitfalls for a One: Rigid and unwilling to change; judgmental; critical

Twos: Twos interact with the world by Striving to Be Connected. They are often selfless, caring, and nurturing. They focus on helping others meet their needs; they build rapport easily and enjoy finding a common bond with others. When they overdo their Striving to Be Connected, they may fail to take care of their own needs and end up becoming emotionally dependent on others. Under stress, Twos may fear that if they are not closely connected to others, they will become isolated.
Pitfalls for a Two: Breaking boundaries; histrionics; always taking support role

Threes: Threes interact with the world by Striving to Be Outstanding. They work hard to exceed standards and to be successful in whatever they undertake. They place high value on productivity and presenting an image of being a winner in whatever environment they are in. When they overdo their Striving to Be Outstanding, they may become attention-seeking and may value image over substance. When stressed, Threes may fear that if they are not making great efforts to be excellent, they will become mediocre.
Pitfalls for a Three: "Yes, I'll Do It" syndrome; spin and wanting to look good; seeking recognition

Fours: Fours interact with the world by Striving to Be Unique. They generally approach their lives creatively, in fresh and interesting ways. They gravitate toward things and experiences that are elegant, refined, or unusual. When they overdo their Striving to Be Unique, they may feel misunderstood and may withdraw from others and become isolated. When stressed, Fours may fear that if they do not put their own special touch on their world and their experiences, their individuality will become repressed.
Pitfalls for a Four: Rebellion for rebellion's sake; insistence on being right; drama

Fives: Fives interact with the world by Striving to Be Detached. They are observant, logical, and generally reserved. They focus on problem solving, innovative ideas, and data gathering. When they overdo their Striving to Be Detached, they can end up being dull—out of touch with their experiences and emotions. When stressed, Fives may fear that if they do not remain detached and guarded, they will become uncontrolled.

Pitfalls for a Five: Thinking too much, doing too little; not nurturing relationships; unaware of surroundings and impact on others

Sixes: Sixes interact with the world by Striving to Be Secure. They find security in being part of something bigger than themselves, such as a group or tradition. They are careful, responsible, and protective of the welfare of the group. They focus on maintaining consistency, tradition, and cohesion. When they overdo their Striving to Be Secure, they may fail to take the risks necessary for high performance and settle for mediocrity. When stressed, Sixes may fear that if they relax their guard, they will be vulnerable to possible dangers.
Pitfalls for a Six: Pessimism; suspicion; "Dog with the Bone" syndrome

Sevens: Sevens interact with the world by Striving to Be Excited. They are upbeat, enthusiastic, optimistic, and curious. They focus on possibilities and options and keeping others entertained. When they overdo their Striving to Be Excited, they may fail to follow through, become easily distracted, and act irresponsibly. When stressed, Sevens may fear that if they do not keep their options open, they will miss out on something.
Pitfalls for a Seven: Talking too much; not following through; avoiding unpleasantness

Eights: Eights interact with the world by Striving to Be Powerful. They are action-oriented self-starters who love to be in charge. They focus on getting things done and overcoming the obstacles that may lie in their way. When they overdo their Striving to Be Powerful, they may not adhere to the rules or norms that others expect them to follow and their behavior can become uncontrolled. When stressed, Eights may fear that if they become too connected to others or experience their own emotions too deeply, they will become dependent on others.
Pitfalls for an Eight: Bullying; always being right; needing to be the boss

Nines: Nines interact with the world by Striving to Be Peaceful. They are calm, pleasant, and likable. They focus on maintaining a sense of inner harmony by minimizing their own needs and concentrating on the needs of others. When they overdo their Striving to Be Peaceful, they can become passive, relying on others to make decisions for them. When stressed, Nines may fear that if they place too much importance on themselves, they will be seen as attention-seeking.
Pitfalls for a Nine: Holding back; avoiding conflict; "The Nice Guy" syndrome

For more information about the Enneagram assessment,
please visit www.enneagramlearning.com.

Appendix B

Inspirational Quotes

(To see these online as well as more,
visit http://KerpenQuotes.com)

On Listening

Wisdom is the reward you get for a lifetime of listening when you'd have preferred to talk. **—Doug Larson**

One of the most sincere forms of respect is actually listening to what another has to say. **—Bryant H. McGill**

If you make listening and observation your occupation, you will gain much more than you can by talk. **—Robert Baden-Powell**

Listening is a magnetic and strange thing, a creative force. The friends who listen to us are the ones we move toward. When we are listened to, it creates us, makes us unfold and expand. **—Karl A. Menninger**

Most of the successful people I've known are the ones who do more listening than talking. **—Bernard Baruch**

There is as much wisdom in listening as there is in speaking—and that goes for all relationships, not just romantic ones. **—Daniel Dae Kim**

The most important thing in communication is hearing what isn't said. **—Peter Drucker**

When people talk, listen completely. Most people never listen. **—Ernest Hemingway**

Most people do not listen with the intent to understand; they listen with the intent to reply. **—Stephen R. Covey**

Friends are those rare people who ask how we are, and then wait to hear the answer. **—Ed Cunningham**

The art of conversation lies in listening. **—Malcolm Forbes**

You cannot truly listen to anyone and do anything else at the same time, **—M. Scott Peck**

We have two ears and one tongue so that we would listen more and talk less. **—Diogenes**

On Storytelling

Stories are a communal currency of humanity. **—Tahir Shah**

Great stories happen to those who can tell them. **—Ira Glass**

The human species thinks in metaphors and learns through stories. **—Mary Catherine Bateson**

Sometimes reality is too complex. Stories give it form. **—Jean-Luc Godard**

If you're going to have a story, have a big story, or none at all. **—Joseph Campbell**

Storytelling reveals meaning without committing the error of defining it. **—Hannah Arendt**

The stories we tell literally make the world. If you want to change the world, you need to change your story. This truth applies both to individuals and institutions. **—Michael Margolis**

Those who tell the stories rule the world. **—Hopi American Indian proverb**

There's always room for a story that can transport people to another place. **—J. K. Rowling**

On Authenticity

Enlightenment is the key to everything, and it is the key to intimacy, because it is the goal of true authenticity. **—Marianne Williamson**

I know of nothing more valuable, when it comes to the all-important virtue of authenticity, than simply being who you are. **—Charles R. Swindoll**

Yes, in all my research, the greatest leaders looked inward and were able to tell a good story with authenticity and passion. **—Deepak Chopra**

Hard times arouse an instinctive desire for authenticity. **—Coco Chanel**

Always be a first-rate version of yourself and not a second-rate version of someone else. **—Judy Garland**

Be yourself—not your idea of what you think somebody else's idea of yourself should be. **—Henry David Thoreau**

Shine with all you have. When someone tries to blow you out, just take their oxygen and burn brighter. **—Katelyn S. Irons**

Live authentically. Why would you continue to compromise something that's beautiful to create something that is fake? **—Steve Maraboli**

Authenticity requires a certain measure of vulnerability, transparency, and integrity **—Janet Louise Stephenson**

We have to dare to be ourselves, however frightening or strange that self may prove to be. **—May Sarton**

I can be a better me than anyone can. **—Diana Ross**

On Transparency

There is no persuasiveness more effectual than the transparency of a single heart, of a sincere life. **—Joseph Barber Lightfoot**

A lack of transparency results in distrust and a deep sense of insecurity. **—Dalai Lama**

I love when things are transparent, free, and clear of all inhibition and judgment. **—Pharrell Williams**

I wish that every human life might be pure transparent freedom. **—Simone de Beauvoir**

Truth never damages a cause that is just. **—Mahatma Gandhi**

Our whole philosophy is one of transparency. **—Valerie Jarrett**

I just think we need more accountability and more transparency. **—John Thune**

Honesty is the first chapter in the book of wisdom. **—Thomas Jefferson**

On Teamwork

Individual commitment to a group effort—that is what makes a team work, a company work, a society work, a civilization work. **—Vince Lombardi**

Talent wins games, but teamwork and intelligence win championships. **—Michael Jordan**

Teamwork is the ability to work together toward a common vision. The ability to direct individual accomplishments toward organizational objectives. It is the fuel that allows common people to attain uncommon results. **—Andrew Carnegie**

Alone we can do so little, together we can do so much. **—Helen Keller**

None of us is as smart as all of us. **—Ken Blanchard**

Coming together is a beginning. Keeping together is progress. Working together is success. **—Henry Ford**

If everyone is moving forward together, then success takes care of itself. **—Henry Ford**

The strength of the team is each individual member. The strength of each member is the team. **—Phil Jackson**

Collaboration allows teachers to capture each other's fund of collective intelligence. **—Mike Schmoker**

It takes two flints to make a fire. **—Louisa May Alcott**

Unity is strength . . . when there is teamwork and collaboration, wonderful things can be achieved. **—Mattie Stepanek**

The best teamwork comes from men who are working independently toward one goal in unison. **—James Cash Penney**

On Responsiveness

Confidence, like art, never comes from having all the answers; it comes from being open to all the questions. **—Earl Gray Stevens**

Life is 10 percent what happens to me and 90 percent how I react. **—John C. Maxwell**

The pessimist complains about the wind; the optimist expects it to change; the realist adjusts the sails. **—William Arthur Ward**

The most difficult thing is the decision to act; the rest is merely tenacity. **—Amelia Earhart**

Either you run the day, or the day runs you **—Jim Rohn**

On Adaptability

It is not the strongest nor the most intelligent who will survive but those who can best manage change. **—Charles Darwin**

Adaptability is about the powerful difference between adapting to cope and adapting to win. **—Max McKeown**

The art of life is a constant readjustment to our surroundings. **—Kakuzo Okakura**

Adaptability is not imitation. It means power of resistance and assimilation. **—Mahatma Gandhi**

People will try to tell you that all the great opportunities have been snapped up. In reality, the world changes every second, blowing new opportunities in all directions, including yours. **—Ken Hakuta**

All fixed set patterns are incapable of adaptability or pliability. The truth is outside of all fixed patterns. **—Bruce Lee**

A wise man adapts himself to circumstances, as water shapes itself to the vessel that contains it. **—Chinese Proverb**

Fall seven times and stand up eight. **—Japanese proverb**

On Passion

There is no passion to be found playing small—in settling for a life that is less than the one you are capable of living. **—Nelson Mandela**

Develop a passion for learning. If you do, you will never cease to grow. **—Anthony J. D'Angelo**

Passion is energy. Feel the power that comes from focusing on what excites you. **—Oprah Winfrey**

We must act out passion before we can feel it. **—Jean-Paul Sartre**

Nothing is as important as passion. No matter what you want to do with your life, be passionate. **—Jon Bon Jovi**

If you feel like there's something out there that you're supposed to be doing, if you have a passion for it, then stop wishing and just do it. **—Wanda Sykes**

If you don't love what you do, you won't do it with much conviction or passion. **—Mia Hamm**

It is the soul's duty to be loyal to its own desires. It must abandon itself to its master passion. **—Rebecca West**

On Surprise and Delight

The husband who decides to surprise his wife is often very much surprised himself. **—Voltaire**

It doesn't take much to surprise others, but to surprise oneself—now that is a great feat. **—Kristen Hartley**

Surprise yourself every day with your own courage. **—Denholm Elliott**

To the issues of friendship, love, business, and war, "surprise" is the optimistic solution. **—Amit Kalantri**

People tend to play in their comfort zone, so the best things are achieved in a state of surprise, actually. **—Brian Eno**

On Simplicity

There is no greatness where there is no simplicity, goodness, and truth. **—Leo Tolstoy**

Manifest plainness, embrace simplicity, reduce selfishness, have few desires. **—Lao Tzu**

Simplicity is the most difficult thing to secure in this world; it is the last limit of experience and the last effort of genius. **—George Sand**

There is a certain majesty in simplicity which is far above all the quaintness of wit. **—Alexander Pope**

If you can't explain it to a six-year-old, you don't understand it yourself. **—Albert Einstein**

Life is really simple, but we insist on making it complicated. **—Aristotle**

Simplicity is about subtracting the obvious and adding the meaningful. **—John Maeda**

Free yourself from the complexities of your life! A life of simplicity and happiness awaits you. **—Steve Maraboli**

On Gratefulness

Reflect upon your present blessings, of which every man has many; not on your past misfortunes, of which all men have some. **—Charles Dickens**

The truest indication of gratitude is to return what you are grateful for. **—Richard Paul Evans**

When you are grateful—when you can see what you have—you unlock blessings to flow in your life. **—Suze Orman**

We must find time to stop and thank the people who make a difference in our lives. **—John F. Kennedy**

You can complain because roses have thorns, or you can be grateful that thornbushes have roses. **—Tom Wilson**

Cultivate the habit of being grateful for every good thing that comes to you, and to give thanks continuously. And because all things have contributed to your advancement, you should include all things in your gratitude. **—Ralph Waldo Emerson**

Let gratitude be the pillow upon which you kneel to say your nightly prayer. And let faith be the bridge you build to overcome evil and welcome good. **—Maya Angelou**

We can only be said to be alive in those moments when our hearts are conscious of our treasures. —**Thornton Wilder**

As we express our gratitude, we must never forget that the highest appreciation is not to utter words, but to live by them. **—John F. Kennedy**

Gratitude is not only the greatest of virtues, but the parent of all others. **—Cicero**

Those who have the ability to be grateful are the ones who have the ability to achieve greatness. **—Steve Maraboli**

On Kindness

This is my simple religion. There is no need for temples; no need for complicated philosophy. Our own brain, our own heart is our temple; the philosophy is kindness. **—Dalai Lama**

A warm smile is the universal language of kindness. **—William Arthur Ward**

There is overwhelming evidence that the higher the level of self-esteem, the more likely one will be to treat others with respect, kindness, and generosity. **—Nathaniel Branden**

Wherever there is a human being, there is an opportunity for a kindness. **—Lucius Annaeus Seneca**

Treat everyone with respect and kindness. Period. No exceptions. **—Kiana Tom**

Be kind, for everyone you meet is fighting a harder battle. **—Plato**

The smallest act of kindness is worth more than the greatest intention. **—Kahlil Gibran**

I would rather make mistakes in kindness and compassion than work miracles in unkindness and hardness. **—Mother Teresa**

Never lose a chance of saying a kind word. **—William Makepeace Thackeray**

Our kindness may be the most persuasive argument for that which we believe. **—Gordon B. Hinckley**

It's a little embarrassing that after forty-five years of research and study, the best advice I can give people is to be a little kinder to each other. **—Aldous Huxley**

It seems to me that no matter what religion you subscribe to, acts of kindness are the stepping-stones to making the world a better place—because we become better people in it. **—Jodi Picoult**

On Humility

Never look down on anybody unless you're helping them up. **—Jesse Jackson**

Pride makes us artificial and humility makes us real. **—Thomas Merton**

Real genius is nothing else but the supernatural virtue of humility in the domain of thought. **—Simone Weil**

Humility is really important, because it keeps you fresh and new. **—Steven Tyler**

Humility, that low, sweet root, from which all heavenly virtues shoot. **—Thomas Moore**

Humility is throwing oneself away in complete concentration on something or someone else. **—Madeleine L'Engle**

Selflessness is humility. Humility and freedom go hand in hand. Only a humble person can be free. **—Jeff Wilson**

On Giving

No one has ever become poor by giving. **—Anne Frank**

A kind gesture can reach a wound that only compassion can heal. **—Steve Maraboli**

As we work to create light for others, we naturally light our own way. **—Mary Anne Radmacher**

Even the smallest act of caring for another person is like a drop of water—it will make ripples throughout the entire pond. . . . **—Jessy and Bryan Matteo**

Don't wait for other people to be loving, giving, compassionate, grateful, forgiving, generous, or friendly . . . lead the way! **—Steve Maraboli**

What we spend, we lose. What we keep will be left for others. What we give away will be ours forever. **—David McGee**

When in doubt as to what you should do, err on the side of giving. **—Tony Cleaver**

Every sunrise is an invitation for us to arise and brighten someone's day. **—Richelle E. Goodrich**

On Persistence

Nothing in the world can take the place of persistence. Talent will not; nothing is more common than unsuccessful men with talent. Genius will not; unrewarded genius is almost a proverb. Education will not; the world is full of educated derelicts. Persistence and determination alone are omnipotent. **—Calvin Coolidge**

Energy and persistence conquer all things. **—Benjamin Franklin**

As long as we are persistence in our pursuit of our deepest destiny, we will continue to grow. We cannot choose the day or time when we will fully bloom. It happens in its own time. **—Denis Waitley**

When I meet successful people I ask 100 questions as to what they attribute their success to. It is usually the same: persistence, hard work, and hiring good people. **—Kiana Tom**

Success is stumbling from failure to failure with no loss of enthusiasm. **—Winston Churchill**

The best way out is always through. **—Robert Frost**

Knowing trees, I understand the meaning of patience. Knowing grass, I can appreciate persistence. **—Hal Borland**

Character consists of what you do on the third and fourth tries. **—James A. Michener**

If you wish to be out front, then act as if you were behind. **—Lao Tzu**

The slogans "hang on" and "press on" have solved and will continue to solve the problems of humanity. **—Ogwo David Emenike**

On Inspiration

Do you want to know who you are? Don't ask. Act! Action will delineate and define you. **—Thomas Jefferson**

The best way to predict the future is to invent it. **—Alan Kay**

I know for sure that what we dwell on is who we become. **—Oprah Winfrey**

Logic will get you from A to B. Imagination will take you everywhere. **—Albert Einstein**

If not us, who? If not now, when? **—Hillel the Elder**

Winners lose much more often than losers. So if you keep losing but you're still trying, keep it up! You're right on track. **—Matthew Keith Groves**

Success is not the key to happiness. Happiness is the key to success. If you love what you are doing, you'll be a success. **—Albert Schweitzer**

When the need to succeed is as bad as the need to breathe, then you'll be successful. **—Eric Thomas**

On Life

In three words I can sum up everything I've learned about life: it goes on. **—Robert Frost**

Go confidently in the direction of your dreams. Live the life you have imagined. **—Henry David Thoreau**

Only a life lived for others is a life worthwhile. **—Albert Einstein**

Life is a succession of lessons which must be lived to be understood. **—Helen Keller**

The price of anything is the amount of life you exchange for it. **—Henry David Thoreau**

Life is far too important a thing ever to talk seriously about. **—Oscar Wilde**

Don't let life discourage you; everyone who got where he is had to begin where he was. **—Richard L. Evans**

The only disability in life is a bad attitude. **—Scott Hamilton**

If you live long enough, you'll make mistakes. But if you learn from them, you'll be a better person. It's how you handle adversity, not how it affects you. The main thing is never quit, never quit, never quit.
—William J. Clinton

On Love

Keep love in your heart. A life without it is like a sunless garden when the flowers are dead. **—Oscar Wilde**

I have decided to stick with love. Hate is too great a burden to bear.
—Martin Luther King Jr.

Where there is love there is life. **—Mahatma Gandhi**

Let us always meet each other with a smile,
for the smile is the beginning of love. **—Mother Teresa**

A loving heart is the beginning of all knowledge. **—Thomas Carlyle**

A flower cannot blossom without sunshine,
and man cannot live without love. **—Max Muller**

Love yourself first and everything else falls into line. You really have to love yourself to get anything done in this world. **—Lucille Ball**

Love is a better teacher than duty. **—Albert Einstein**

Love is life. And if you miss love, you miss life. **—Leo Buscaglia**

On Change

Be the change that you wish to see in the world. **—Mahatma Gandhi**

Never doubt that a small group of thoughtful, committed citizens can change the world. Indeed, it is the only thing that ever has.
—Margaret Mead

Everyone thinks of changing the world, but no one
thinks of changing himself. **—Leo Tolstoy**

Education is the most powerful weapon which you can use to change the world. **—Nelson Mandela**

Change the way you look at things and the things you look at change.
—Wayne W. Dyer

No matter who you are, no matter what you did, no matter where you've come from, you can always change, become a better version of yourself.
—Madonna

Those who cannot change their minds cannot change anything.
—George Bernard Shaw

I alone cannot change the world, but I can cast a stone across the waters to create many ripples. **—Mother Teresa**

To improve is to change; to be perfect is to change often.
—Winston Churchill

A tiny change today brings a dramatically different tomorrow.
—Richard Bach

Change your thoughts and you change your world.
—Norman Vincent Peale

On Letting Go

Forgiveness does not change the past, but it does enlarge the future.
—Paul Boese

Some people believe holding on and hanging in there are signs of great strength. However, there are times when it takes much more strength to know when to let go and then do it. **—Ann Landers**

The beautiful journey of today can only begin when we learn to let go of yesterday. **—Steve Maraboli**

Thank God I found the GOOD in goodbye. **—Beyoncé Knowles**

The weak can never forgive. Forgiveness is the attribute of the strong.
—Mahatma Gandhi

Always forgive your enemies—nothing annoys them so much.
—Oscar Wilde

When you forgive, you in no way change the past—but you sure do change the future. **—Bernard Meltzer**

To err is human; to forgive, divine. **—Alexander Pope**

Forgiveness is a gift you give yourself. **—Suzanne Somers**

Without forgiveness, there's no future. **—Desmond Tutu**

Sooner or later we've all got to let go of our past. **—Dan Brown**

Yesterday is not ours to recover, but tomorrow is ours to win or lose.
—Lyndon B. Johnson

The great courageous act that we must all do is to have the courage to step out of our history and past so that we can live our dreams.
—Oprah Winfrey

On Family

The love of family and the admiration of friends is much more important than wealth and privilege. **—Charles Kuralt**

Family is not an important thing. It's everything. **—Michael J. Fox**

Family is the most important thing in the world. **—Princess Diana**

A happy family is but an earlier heaven. **—George Bernard Shaw**

A man should never neglect his family for business. **—Walt Disney**

Cherish your human connections—your relationships with friends and family. **—Barbara Bush**

In every conceivable manner, the family is link to our past, bridge to our future. **—Alex Haley**

The family is one of nature's masterpieces. **—George Santayana**

Family means no one gets left behind or forgotten. **—David Ogden Stiers**

A man travels the world over in search of what he needs, and returns home to find it. **—George Moore**

I sustain myself with the love of family. **—Maya Angelou**

On Strength and Courage

That which does not kill us makes us stronger. **—Friedrich Nietzsche**

Courage is the most important of all the virtues, because without courage, you can't practice any other virtue consistently. **—Maya Angelou**

Strength does not come from physical capacity. It comes from an indomitable will. **—Mahatma Gandhi**

With the new day comes new strength and new thoughts. **—Eleanor Roosevelt**

Be strong. Live honorably and with dignity. When you don't think you can, hold on. **—James Frey**

My attitude is that if you push me towards something that you think is a weakness, then I will turn that perceived weakness into a strength. **—Michael Jordan**

We gain strength, and courage, and confidence by each experience in which we really stop to look fear in the face . . . we must do that which we think we cannot. **—Eleanor Roosevelt**

On Leadership

Leadership is service, not position. **—Tim Fargo**

A leader is a dealer in hope. **—Napoleon Bonaparte**

A leader is one who knows the way, goes the way, and shows the way. **—John C. Maxwell**

As we look ahead into the next century, leaders will be those who empower others. **—Bill Gates**

A genuine leader is not a searcher for consensus but a molder of consensus. **—Martin Luther King Jr.**

Leaders think and talk about the solutions. Followers think and talk about the problems. **—Brian Tracy**

Leadership and learning are indispensable to each other. **—John F. Kennedy**

To handle yourself, use your head; to handle others, use your heart. **—Eleanor Roosevelt**

Management is nothing more than motivating other people. **—Lee Iacocca**

Management is efficiency in climbing the ladder of success; leadership determines whether the ladder is leaning against the right wall. **—Stephen Covey**

The key to successful leadership today is influence, not authority. **—Kenneth Blanchard**

On Legacy

Carve your name on hearts, not tombstones. A legacy is etched into the minds of others and the stories they share about you. **—Shannon L. Alder**

If you would not be forgotten as soon as you are dead, either write something worth reading or do something worth writing. **—Benjamin Franklin**

The things you do for yourself are gone when you are gone, but the things you do for others remain as your legacy. **—Kalu Ndukwe Kalu**

The greatest use of life is to spend it for something that will outlast it. **—William James**

You can't leave a footprint that lasts if you're always walking on tiptoe. **—Marion Blake**